365 Easy Slow Cooker Recipes

HB
HINKLER
BOOKS

Cover by Nancy Bohanan
Illustrations by Nancy Murphy Griffith
Pre-press by Graphic Print Group

365 Easy Slow Cooker Recipes
Published in 2009 by Hinkler Books Pty Ltd
45–55 Fairchild Street
Heatherton VIC 3202 Australia
www.hinklerbooks.com
This edition published in 2010 for Index Books Ltd

© Cookbook Resources, LLC 2008

10 9 8 7 6 5
14 13 12 11 10

All rights reserved. No part of this publication may be reproduced, stored in
a retrieval system, or transmitted in any way or by any means, electronic, mechanical,
photocopying, recording or otherwise, without the prior written permission of the
copyright holders.

ISBN: 978 1 7418 3132 0
Printed and bound in China

Introduction

These convenient slow cookers make life easier for anyone who uses them. Put your food inside, cover the pot, turn the switch to 'on' and come home after hours of errands, soccer games, meetings, work or play and dinner is ready! Meals are simple, convenient and much healthier than any fast-food meal.

365 Easy Slow Cooker Recipes provides recipes for beef, chicken, seafood, vegetables, soups and casseroles that are great as one-dish meals or as accompaniments to a main dish.

These recipes are family tested and used every day by mums, dads, seniors, teens and university students. They are nutritious, economical, wholesome and practical, and are ones families grew up on and remember long after adulthood. They are recipes that give you a warm and fuzzy feeling and let you know someone cares about you.

These recipes should never be taken for granted or passed by because they are too simple or too 'normal'. They are recipes that strengthen families and bring them the happiness and satisfaction of being together for a home-cooked meal.

Cooking is one of life's simple pleasures. And these recipes make it easy to enjoy quality time with people you care about.

Contents

Contents

Dedication

With a mission of helping you bring family and friends to the table, this book aims to make family meals and cooking for friends simple, easy and delicious.

We recognise the importance of a meal together as a means of building family bonds with memories and traditions that will be treasured for a lifetime. It is an opportunity to sit down with each other and share more than food.

This cookbook is dedicated with gratitude and respect to all those who show their love with homecooked meals, bringing family and friends to the table.

More and more statistical studies are finding that family meals play a significant role in childhood development. Children who eat with their families four or more nights per week are healthier, attain higher marks at school, score higher on aptitude tests and are less likely to have problems with drugs.

Appetisers

Dips, Spreads,
Wings & Things

Appetisers Contents

Unbelievable Crab Dip

1 170-g (6-ounce) can crabmeat, drained, flaked
230 g (8 ounces) cream cheese, softened
½ cup (115 g) butter, sliced
2 tablespoons (30 ml) white cooking wine

- Combine crabmeat, cream cheese, butter and wine in small, sprayed slow cooker.

- Cover and cook on low for 1 hour and gently stir to combine all ingredients. Serve from cooker with chips or crackers. Serves 4 to 6.

Crab Dip

230 g (8 ounces) and 85 g (3 ounces) cream cheese, softened
⅔ cup (150 g) mayonnaise
1 tablespoon (15 ml) Worcestershire sauce
1 tablespoon (15 ml) sherry or cooking sherry
3 fresh spring onions with tops, chopped
2 170-g (6-ounce) cans crabmeat, drained, flaked

- Combine cream cheese, mayonnaise, 1 teaspoon salt and Worcestershire sauce in bowl and mix well with fork.

- Stir in sherry, onions and crabmeat and spoon into small, sprayed slow cooker.

- Cover and cook on low for 1 hour 30 minutes to 2 hours and stir once. Serves 6 to 8.

Broccoli Dip

¾ cup (170 g) butter
2 cups (200 g) thinly sliced celery
1 onion, finely chopped
3 tablespoons (20 g) flour
1 280-g (10-ounce) can cream of
   chicken soup
280 g (10 ounces) frozen chopped
   broccoli florets, thawed
145 g (5 ounces) garlic cheese, cut
   in chunks
Crackers or corn chips

- Melt butter in frypan and sauté celery and onion, but do not brown. Stir in flour.

- Spoon into small slow cooker, stir in remaining ingredients and mix well.

- Cover and cook on low for 2 to 3 hours and stir several times.

- Serve with crackers or corn chips. Serves 6 to 8.

Hot Southwest Dip

680 g (1½ pounds) lean minced
   beef
2 onions, finely diced
280 g (10 ounces) can diced
   tomatoes
2 chopped green chillies
1 230-g (8-ounce) can tomato
   soup
455 g (16 ounces) shredded
   cheese
Corn chips

- Cook beef and onions in large frypan until onions are translucent. Drain and transfer to sprayed slow cooker. Add tomatoes, green chillies, tomato soup and cheese. Stir until they blend well.

- Cover and cook on low for 2 hours, stirring every 30 minutes. Use chips for dipping. Serves 12 to 14.

Cheesy Bacon Dip

2 230-g (8-ounce) packets cream cheese, softened
230 g (8 ounces) Colby cheese, shredded
2 tablespoons (30 ml) mustard
2 teaspoons Worcestershire sauce
4 fresh spring onions with tops, sliced
455 g (1 pound) bacon, cooked, crumbled
Rye or pumpernickel bread

- Cut cream cheese into cubes and place in 4 to 5-L (4 to 5-quart) slow cooker.

- Add cheese, mustard, Worcestershire sauce, spring onions and ¼ teaspoon (1 ml) salt.

- Cover and cook on low for 1 hour and stir to melt cheese.

- Stir in crumbled bacon. Serve with small-size rye bread or toasted pumpernickel bread. Serves 6 to 8.

Hamburger Dip

Men love this meaty, spicy dip.

**910 g (2 pounds) lean minced
    beef
2 tablespoons (30 ml) minced
    onion
1½ teaspoons dried oregano
    leaves
1 tablespoon (15 ml) chilli
    powder
2 teaspoons sugar
1 280-g (10-ounce) can tomatoes
2 chopped green chillies
½ cup chilli sauce (135 g)
2 455-g (16-ounce) cubed Tasty
    cheese
Chips or crackers**

- Brown beef in large frypan, drain and transfer to sprayed 4 to 5-L (4 to 5-quart) slow cooker.

- Add remaining ingredients plus ½ to 1 cup (125 to 250 ml) water and stir well.

- Cover and cook on low for 1 hour 30 minutes to 2 hours. Stir once or twice during cooking time. Add a little salt, if desired. Serve hot with chips or spread on crackers.
  Serves 8 to 10.

Hot Broccoli Dip

455 g (16 ounces) Tasty cheese, cubed
1 teaspoon paprika
280 g (10 ounces) can mushroom soup
¼ cup (60 ml) milk
280 g (10 ounces) frozen chopped broccoli florets, thawed

- Combine cheese, paprika, soup and milk in sprayed slow cooker, stir well and fold in broccoli.

- Cover and cook on low for 1 to 2 hours. Stir before serving. Serves 8 to 10.

Mexican-Corn Dip

455 g (1 pound) lean minced beef
1 onion, finely chopped
1 425-g (15-ounce) can corn kernels, drained
1 455-g (16-ounce) jar salsa
455 g (1 pound) cubed Tasty cheese
Corn chips

- Brown and cook beef in frypan on low heat for about 10 minutes and drain.

- Transfer to slow cooker and add onion, corn, salsa and cheese.

- Cover and cook on low for 1 hour, remove lid and stir. Serve with corn chips. Serves 6 to 8.

Chicken-Enchilada Dip

910 g (2 pounds) boneless,
  skinless chicken thighs, cubed
1 280-g (10-ounce) can
  enchilada sauce
2 chopped green chillies
1 small onion, finely chopped
1 large red capsicum, seeded,
  finely chopped
460 g (16 ounces) cream cheese,
  cubed
455 g (16 ounces) shredded
  Cheddar cheese
Corn chips

- Place chicken thighs, enchilada sauce, green chillies, onion and capsicum in sprayed 4 to 5-L (4 to 5-quart) slow cooker.

- Cover and cook on low for 4 to 6 hours. Stir in cream cheese and Cheddar cheese and cook an additional 30 minutes.

- Stir several times during cooking. Serve with corn chips. Serves 8 to 10.

Salami Dip

170 g (6 ounces) salami
1 bunch fresh spring onions,
thinly sliced
½ red capsicum, finely chopped
1 medium tomato, finely chopped
1 400-g (14-ounce) jar pizza
sauce
1½ cups (170 g) shredded
mozzarella cheese
230 g (8 ounces) cream cheese,
cubed
Crackers or corn chips

- Chop salami into small pieces and place in small slow cooker.

- Add onion, capsicum, tomato and pizza sauce and stir well.

- Cover and cook on low for 2 hours 30 minutes to 3 hours 30 minutes.

- Stir in mozzarella and cream cheese and stir until they melt.

- Serve with wheat crackers or corn chips. Serves 4 to 6.

Sausage-Hamburger Dip

**455 g (1 pound) bulk pork
  sausage meat
455 g (1 pound) lean minced beef
1 cup (265 g) hot salsa
1 280-g (10-ounce) can cream of
  mushroom soup
1 280-g (10-ounce) can tomatoes
2 chopped green chillies
1 teaspoon garlic powder
¾ teaspoon ground oregano
2 455-g (16-ounce) cubed
  cheddar cheese**

- Cook sausage and beef in large frypan for 15 minutes and drain.

- Place in sprayed 4 to 5-L (4 to 5-quart) slow cooker.

- Add salsa, mushroom soup, tomatoes, green chillies, garlic powder and oregano, stir well. Fold in cheese.

- Cover and cook on low for 1 hour or until cheese melts. Stir once during cooking time.

- Serve from cooker. Serves 8 to 10.

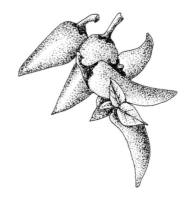

Whiz Bang Dip

455 g (1 pound) lean minced beef
1 small onion, very finely
    chopped
910 g (32 ounces) cubed cheddar
    cheese
2 280-g (10-ounce) cans chopped
    tomatoes
4 chopped green chillies
1 teaspoon minced garlic
Corn chips

- Cook beef in frypan on low heat
  for 10 minutes and break up
  large meat chunks. Transfer to
  4-L (4-quart) slow cooker and
  add onion, cheese, tomatoes,
  green chillies and garlic.

- Stir well, cover and cook on
  low for 1 hour. Serve with corn
  chips. Serves 6 to 8.

The Big Dipper

2 425-g (15-ounce) cans
    chilli
1 280-g (10-ounce) can tomatoes
2 chopped green chillies
1 455-g (16-ounces) packet cubed
    cheddar cheese
1 bunch fresh spring onions,
    chopped

- Place all ingredients in slow
  cooker. Cover and cook on low
  for 1 hour to 1 hour 30 minutes.

- Serve right from slow cooker.
  Stir before serving. Serves 6
  to 8.

Firecrackers and Bacon

455 g (16 ounces) cubed cheddar
    cheese
1 280-g (10-ounce) can tomatoes
2 green chillies, chopped
1 tablespoon (15 ml) minced
    onion
2 teaspoons Worcestershire sauce
½ teaspoon mustard
½ cup (125 ml) unthickened
    cream
16 slices bacon, cooked, crumbled

- Combine cubed cheese, tomatoes, green chillies, onion, Worcestershire sauce, mustard and cream to small, sprayed slow cooker.

- Turn heat to low, cover and cook for about 1 hour, stirring several times to make sure cheese melts.

- While cheese is melting, place bacon in frypan, fry, drain and crumble.

- Fold three-fourths of bacon into cheese mixture. When ready to 'dip', sprinkle remaining bacon on top and serve from slow cooker. Serves 4 to 6.

Great Balls of Fire

455 g (1 pound) hot sausage meat
280 g (10 ounces) tomatoes,
**   chopped**
2 green chillies, chopped
910 g (2 pounds) cheese

- Brown and cook sausage in frypan, drain and place in small, sprayed slow cooker.

- Stir in tomatoes, green chillies and mix well.

- Cut cheese into chunks and add to sausage-tomato mixture.

- Cover and cook on low for 1 hour or until cheese melts.

- Stir when ready to serve and serve hot in slow cooker. Serves 4 to 6.

TIP: This works best with large corn chips.

Hot Reuben Spread

230 g (8 ounces) shredded Swiss
**   cheese**
¾ cup (110 g) sauerkraut, rinsed,
**   drained**
230 g (8 ounces) cream cheese,
**   softened, cubed**
140 g (5 ounces) sliced
**   corned beef, chopped**

- Combine Swiss cheese, sauerkraut, cream cheese and corned beef in bowl and spoon into small, sprayed slow cooker.

- Cover and cook on low for 1 hour.

- Serve on slices of 8-cm (3-inch) rye bread. Serves 4 to 6.

Crab-Artichoke Spread

1 170-g (6-ounce) can crabmeat,
  flaked
½ cup (50 g) grated parmesan
  cheese
1 bunch fresh spring onions,
  sliced
1½ tablespoons (22 ml) lemon
  juice
1 425-g (15-ounce) can artichoke
  hearts, drained, finely
  chopped
230 g (8 ounces) cream cheese,
  cubed
Toasted bagel chips

- Combine all ingredients in
  small, sprayed slow cooker and
  stir well.

- Cover and cook on low for
  1 hour to 1 hour 30 minutes. Stir
  until cream cheese mixes well.
  Serve on toasted bagel chips.
  Serves 4 to 6.

Party Frankfurters

1 cup (270 g) tomato sauce
1 cup (320 g) plum jam
1 tablespoon (15 ml) lemon
  juice
290 g (10 ounces) tiny smoked
  sausages

- Combine all ingredients in
  small, sprayed slow cooker.

- Cover and cook on low
  for 1 hour.

- Stir before serving. Serve right
  from cooker. Serves 4 to 6.

Sausage-Pineapple Bits

*The 'sweet and hot'
makes a delicious combo.*

**455 g (1 pound) cooked Polish
  sausages, skinned**
**455 g (1 pound) hot bulk sausage
  meat**
**230 g (8 ounces) crushed
  pineapple with juice**
1 cup (320 g) apricot jam
**1 tablespoon (15 ml)
  Worcestershire sauce**
1½ cups (330 g) brown sugar

- Slice sausages into 1.2-cm (½-inch) pieces. Shape bulk sausage into 2.5-cm (1-inch) balls and brown in frypan.

- Combine sausage pieces, sausage balls, pineapple, apricot jam, Worcestershire sauce and brown sugar in slow cooker. Stir gently so meatballs do not break up.

- Cover and cook on low for 1 hour 30 minutes to 2 hours. Serves 8 to 10.

Teriyaki Wings

1.1 kg (2½ pounds) chicken wings
1 onion, chopped
1 cup (250 ml) soy sauce
1 cup (220 g) brown sugar
1 teaspoon minced garlic
1½ teaspoons ground ginger

- Rinse chicken and pat dry. Place chicken wings on griller pan and grill for about 10 minutes on both sides.

- Transfer wings to large slow cooker.

- Combine onion, soy sauce, brown sugar, garlic and ginger in bowl. Spoon sauce over wings.

- Cover and cook on high for 2 hours. Stir wings once during cooking to coat chicken evenly with sauce. Serves 8 to 10.

Wings in Honey Sauce

910 g (2 pounds) chicken wings
2 cups (680 g) honey
¾ cup (175 ml) soy sauce
¾ cup (205 g) chilli sauce
¼ cup (60 ml) canola oil
1 teaspoon minced garlic
Dried parsley flakes

- Rinse chicken, pat dry and sprinkle with a little salt and pepper.

- Place chicken in griller pan and grill for 20 minutes (10 minutes on each side) or until light brown.

- Transfer to sprayed slow cooker.

- Combine honey, soy sauce, chilli sauce, oil and garlic in bowl and spoon over wings.

- Cover and cook on low for 4 to 5 hours or on high for 2 hours to 2 hours 30 minutes. Garnish with dried parsley flakes, if desired. Serves 8 to 10.

Spicy Franks

1 cup (220 g) brown sugar
1 cup (270 g) chilli sauce
1 tablespoon (15 ml) red
**　　wine vinegar**
2 teaspoons soy sauce
2 teaspoons Dijon-style mustard
680 g (24 ounces) frankfurters

- Combine brown sugar, chilli sauce, vinegar, soy sauce and mustard in small, sprayed slow cooker and mix well. Cut frankfurters diagonally in 2.5-cm (1-inch) pieces. Stir in frankfurters.

- Cover and cook on low for 1 to 2 hours.

- Serve from cooker using toothpicks. Serves 4.

Bubbly Franks

455 g (1 pound) wieners
½ cup (135 g) chilli sauce
⅔ cup (150 g) brown sugar
½ cup (125 ml) bourbon

- Cut wieners diagonally into bite-size pieces. Combine chilli sauce, brown sugar and bourbon in small slow cooker.

- Stir in wieners. Cover and cook on low for 1 to 2 hours.

- Serve in chafing dish. Serves 6 to 8.

Soup's On!

*Soups, Stews,
Chowders & Jambalayas*

Soup's On! Contents

Soup's On! Contents

Potato Soup Plus!

5 medium potatoes, peeled, cubed
2 cups (280 g) cooked, cubed ham
1 cup (70 g) fresh broccoli florets,
    finely cut
2 280-g (10-ounce) cans cream of
    celery soup
½ litre (14 ounces) carton chicken
    stock
2½ soup cans filled with milk
Paprika

- Place potatoes, ham and broccoli in sprayed slow cooker.

- Combine soups and milk in saucepan. Heat just enough to mix until smooth. Stir into ingredients already in slow cooker.

- Cover and cook on low for 7 to 9 hours.

- When serving, sprinkle a little paprika over each serving. Serves 6 to 8.

Mexican-Meatball Soup

1½ litres beef stock
1 455-g (16-ounce) jar hot salsa
455 g (16 ounces) frozen corn
    kernels, thawed
455 g (16 ounces) frozen
    meatballs, thawed
1 teaspoon minced garlic

- Combine all ingredients in slow cooker and stir well.

- Cover and cook on low for 5 to 7 hours. Serves 6 to 8.

Tasty Chicken and Rice Soup

**455 g (1 pound) boneless,
  skinless chicken breasts**
½ cup (95 g) brown rice
**1 280-g (10-ounce) can cream
  of chicken soup**
**1 280-g (10-ounce) can cream
  of celery soup**
**½ litre (14 ounces) carton chicken
  stock**
**455 g (16 ounces) frozen sliced
  carrots, thawed**
**1 cup (250 ml) unthickened
  cream**

- Cut chicken into 2.5-cm (1-inch) pieces. Place pieces in sprayed 4 to 5-L (4 to 5-quart) slow cooker.

- Combine and mix rice, soups, chicken stock and carrots in bowl and pour over chicken.

- Cover and cook on low 7 to 8 hours.

- Turn heat to high, add cream and cook an additional 15 to 20 minutes. Serves 6 to 8.

Taco Soup

**680 g (1½ pounds) lean minced
  beef**
30 g (1 ounce) taco seasoning
**2 425-g (15-ounce) cans stewed
  tomatoes**
**2 425-g (15-ounce) cans chilli
  beans with liquid**
**1 425-g (15-ounce) can corn
  kernels, drained**
Crushed corn chips
Shredded cheddar cheese

- Brown beef in frypan until it is
  no longer pink. Place in 5 to 6-L
  (5 to 6-quart) slow cooker.

- Add taco seasoning, tomatoes,
  chilli beans, corn and 1 cup
  (250 ml) water and mix well.

- Cover and cook on low for
  4 hours or on high for
  1 to 2 hours.

- Serve over crushed corn chips
  and sprinkle some shredded
  cheddar cheese over top of each
  serving. Serves 6 to 8.

Taco Soup Olé

**910 g (2 pounds) lean minced
   beef
2 425-g (15-ounce) cans chilli
   beans with liquid
1 425-g (15-ounce) can
   corn kernels, drained
3 425-g (15-ounce) cans
   stewed tomatoes
2 green chillies, chopped
10 g (.04 ounce) French onion
   soup mix
30 g (1 ounce) taco seasoning
Shredded cheddar cheese**

- Brown beef in large frypan, drain and transfer to slow cooker.

- Add remaining ingredients and stir well.

- Cover and cook on low for 8 to 10 hours.

- When serving, sprinkle cheese over each serving. Serves 6 to 8.

Taco-Chilli Soup

**910 g (2 pounds) very lean stew
      meat
2 425-g (15-ounce) cans
      stewed tomatoes
30 g (1 ounce) taco seasoning mix
2 425-g (15-ounce) cans borlotti
      beans with liquid
425 g (15 ounces) can corn
      kernels with liquid
Spring onions, chopped**

- Cut large pieces of stew meat in half and brown in large frypan.

- Combine stew meat, tomatoes, taco seasoning mix, beans, corn and ¾ cup (175 ml) water in 4 to 5-L (4 to 5-quart) slow cooker. (If you are into 'spicy', add a teaspoon of chilli sauce.)

- Cover and cook on low for 5 to 7 hours. Garnish each serving with chopped spring onions. Serves 6 to 8.

Spicy Sausage Soup

**455 g (1 pound) mild bulk
    sausage meat**
**455 g (1 pound) hot bulk sausage
    meat**
**2 425-g (15-ounce) cans stewed
    tomatoes**
2 teaspoons hot chilli sauce
3 cups (305 g) chopped celery
1 cup (120 g) sliced carrots
**1 425-g (15-ounce) can cut green
    beans, drained**
**½ litre (14 ounces) carton
    chicken stock**
1 teaspoon seasoned salt

- Combine mild and hot sausage meat, shape into small balls and place in non-stick frypan. Brown thoroughly and drain.

- Place in large, sprayed slow cooker.

- Add remaining ingredients plus 1 cup (250 ml) water and stir gently so meatballs will not break up.

- Cover and cook on low 6 to 7 hours. Serves 6 to 8.

Tortilla Soup

**3 large boneless, skinless
    chicken breast halves, cubed**
**280 g (10 ounces) frozen corn
    kernels, thawed**
1 onion, chopped
1½ litres chicken stock
**1 170-g (6-ounce) can
    tomato paste**
2 280-g (10-ounce) cans tomatoes
2 green chillies, chopped
2 teaspoons ground cumin
1 teaspoon chilli powder
1 teaspoon minced garlic
6 corn tortillas

- Combine chicken cubes, corn, onion, stock, tomato paste, tomatoes, green chillies, cumin, chilli powder, 1 teaspoon (5 ml) salt and garlic in large slow cooker.

- Cover and cook on low for 5 to 7 hours or on high for 3 hours to 3 hours 30 minutes.

- Preheat oven to 190° C (375° F).

- While soup is cooking, cut tortillas into 6-mm (¼-inch) strips and place on baking tray.

- Bake for about 5 minutes or until crisp.

- Serve baked tortilla strips with soup. Serves 6 to 8.

Southern Soup

1½ cups (360 g) dried
    black-eyed peas
2–3 cups (280–420 g) cooked,
    cubed ham
1 425-g (15-ounce) can
    corn kernels
3 cut okra
1 onion, chopped
1 large potato, cut into small
    cubes
2 teaspoons Cajun seasoning
½ litre (14 ounces) carton
    chicken stock
2 425-g (15-ounce) cans stewed
    tomatoes
2 teaspoons hot chilli sauce

- Rinse peas and drain. Combine peas and 5 cups (1.2 L) water in large saucepan.

- Bring to the boil, reduce heat, simmer for about 10 minutes and drain.

- Combine peas, ham, corn, okra, onion, potato, seasoning, stock and 2 cups (500 ml) water in 5 to 6-L (5 to 6-quart) slow cooker.

- Cover and cook on low for 6 to 8 hours.

- Add stewed tomatoes and chilli sauce, and continue cooking for an additional 1 hour. Serves 6 to 8.

Saucy Cabbage Soup

455 g (1 pound) lean minced beef
1 small head cabbage, chopped
2 425-g (15-ounce) cans borlotti
    beans with liquid
1 425-g (15-ounce) can
    tomato soup
1 425-g (15-ounce) can
    stewed tomatoes
½ litre (14 ounces) carton
    beef stock
2 teaspoons ground cumin

- Brown beef in frypan, drain and place in 5 to 6-L (5 to 6-quart) slow cooker.

- Add cabbage, beans, tomato soup, tomatoes, stock, cumin and 1 cup (250 ml) water and mix well.

- Cover and cook on low for 5 to 6 hours or until cabbage is tender. Serves 4 to 6.

Soup with a Zip

2 425-g (15-ounce) cans stewed
    tomatoes
2 teaspoons hot chilli sauce
1 litre carton chicken stock
2 280-g (10-ounce) cans chicken
    noodle soup
1 425-g (15-ounce) can corn
    kernels, drained
1 425-g (15-ounce) can cut green
    beans, drained
Shredded Tasty cheese

- Place all ingredients except cheese in 4 to 5-L (4 to 5-quart) slow cooker and mix well.

- Cover and cook on low for 2 to 3 hours. When ready to serve, sprinkle shredded cheese over each bowl of soup.
Serves 4 to 6.

Potato and Leek Soup

30 g (1 ounce) white sauce mix
795 g (28 ounces) frozen hash
**   browns**
3 medium leeks, sliced
3 cups (420 g) cooked, cubed ham
1 340-g (12-ounce) can
**   evaporated milk**
230 g (8 ounces) sour cream

- Pour 3 cups (750 ml) water in 4 to 5-L (4 to 5-quart) slow cooker and stir white sauce until smooth.

- Add hash browns, leeks, ham and evaporated milk.

- Cover and cook on low for 7 to 9 hours or on high for 3 hours 30 minutes to 4 hours 30 minutes.

- When ready to serve, turn heat to high. Take out about 2 cups (500 ml) hot soup and pour into separate bowl. Stir in sour cream and return to cooker.

- Cover and cook for an additional 15 minutes or until mixture is thoroughly hot. Serves 6 to 8.

Pork and Beans Soup

910 g (2 pounds) pork shoulder
1 onion, chopped
2 sticks celery, sliced
2 425-g (15-ounce) cans
    cannellini beans with liquid
2 425-g (15-ounce) cans
    stewed tomatoes
1 litre carton chicken stock
1½ teaspoons ground cumin
Flour tortillas
Shredded cheese
Spring onions, chopped

- Cut pork into 1.2-cm (½-inch) cubes.

- Sprinkle pork cubes with a little salt and pepper and brown in frypan.

- Place in 5 to 6-L (5 to 6-quart) slow cooker.

- Combine onion, celery, beans, stewed tomatoes, cumin and 1 cup (250 ml) water in bowl.

- Pour over pork cubes.

- Cover and cook on high for 6 to 7 hours.

- Serve with warmed, buttered tortillas and top each bowl of soup with some shredded cheese and chopped spring onions. Serves 6 to 8.

Pizza Soup

**3 280-g (10-ounce) cans tomato
condensed soup
1 280-g (10-ounce) can French
onion soup
2 teaspoons Italian seasoning
¾ cup (80 g) tiny pasta shells
1½ cups (170 g) shredded
mozzarella cheese**

- Combine soups, Italian
  seasoning and 1½ soup cans
  water in 4 to 5-L (4 to 5-quart)
  slow cooker. Cover and cook on
  high for 1 hour or until mixture
  is hot.

- Add pasta shells and cook for
  1 hour 30 minutes to 2 hours or
  until pasta is cooked.

- Stir several times to keep pasta
  from sticking to bottom of
  slow cooker.

- Turn heat off, add mozzarella
  cheese and stir until cheese
  melts. Serves 6 to 8.

*TIP: For a special way to serve
this soup, sprinkle some
fried onions over top of each
serving.*

Pasta-Veggie Soup

2 yellow squash, chopped
2 zucchini, sliced
280 g (10 ounces) frozen corn
  kernels, thawed
1 red capsicum, chopped
1 425-g (15-ounce) can
  stewed tomatoes
1 teaspoon Italian seasoning
2 teaspoons dried oregano
1 litre carton beef stock
¾ cup (80 g) small pasta shells
Shredded mozzarella cheese

- Combine squash, zucchini, corn, capsicum, tomatoes, Italian seasoning, oregano, stock and 2 cups (500 ml) water in 6-L (6-quart) slow cooker.

- Cover and cook on low for 6 to 7 hours.

- Add pasta shells and cook an additional 30 to 45 minutes or until pasta is tender.

- Garnish with a sprinkle of shredded mozzarella cheese on each bowl of soup. Serves 4 to 5.

Cannellini Bean Soup

8 slices thick-cut bacon
1 carrot
3 425-g (15-ounce) cans
**   cannellini beans with liquid**
3 sticks celery, chopped
1 onion, chopped
1 litre carton chicken stock
1 teaspoon Italian herb seasoning
1 280-g (10-ounce) can cream of
**   chicken soup**

- Cook bacon in frypan, drain and crumble. (Reserve 2 crumbled slices for garnish.)

- Cut carrot in half lengthwise and slice.

- Combine most of crumbled bacon, carrot, beans, celery, onion, stock, seasoning, 1 cup (250 ml) water in 5 to 6-L (5 to 6-quart) slow cooker and stir to mix.

- Cover and cook on low for 5 to 6 hours.

- Ladle 2 cups (500 ml) soup mixture into food processor or blender and process until smooth.

- Return to cooker, add cream of chicken soup and stir to mix.

- Turn heat to high and cook for additional 10 to 15 minutes. Serves 6 to 8.

Meatball Soup

**910 g (32 ounces) frozen
    meatballs, thawed
2 425-g (15-ounce) cans
    stewed tomatoes
3 large potatoes, peeled, diced
4 carrots, peeled, sliced
2 medium onions, chopped
½ litre carton beef stock
2 tablespoons (15 g) cornflour**

- Combine meatballs, tomatoes, potatoes, carrots, onions, beef stock, a little salt and pepper and 1 cup (250 ml) water in sprayed 6-L (6-quart) slow cooker.

- Cover and cook on low for 5 to 6 hours.

- Turn heat to high and combine cornflour with ¼ cup (60 ml) water in bowl. Pour into cooker and cook for an additional 10 or 15 minutes or until slightly thick. Serves 4 to 6.

Borlotti Bean-Vegetable Soup

4 425-g (15-ounce) cans borlotti
   beans with liquid
2 onions, chopped
1 red capsicum, chopped
1 green capsicum, chopped
2 cups (200 g) chopped celery
1 litre carton chicken stock
1 teaspoon Cajun seasoning
⅛ teaspoon cayenne pepper

- Place all ingredients plus 1 cup
  (250 ml) water in 5-L (5-quart)
  slow cooker and stir well.

- Cover and cook on low
  5 to 6 hours. Serves 6 to 8.

Delicious Broccoli-Cheese Soup

455 g (16 ounces) frozen chopped
   broccoli florets, thawed
340 g (12 ounces) cubed cheddar
   cheese
60 g (2 ounces) white sauce mix
30 g (1 ounce) vegetable soup mix
1 340-g (12-ounce) can
   evaporated milk
½ litre carton chicken stock

- Combine all ingredients plus
  2 cups (500 ml) water in large,
  sprayed slow cooker and
  stir well.

- Cover and cook on low for
  6 to 7 hours or on high for
  3 hours 30 minutes to 4 hours.

- Stir frequently 1 hour before
  serving time. Serves 4 to 6.

Italian Bean Soup

2 425-g (15-ounce) cans
    cannellini beans with liquid
2 425-g (15-ounce) cans borlotti
    beans with liquid
1 large onion, chopped
2 beef stock cubes
1 tablespoon (15 ml) minced
    garlic
2 teaspoons Italian seasoning
2 425-g (15-ounce) cans Italian
    stewed tomatoes
1 425-g (15-ounce) can cut
    green beans, drained

- Combine beans, onion, stock cubes, garlic, Italian seasoning and 2 cups (500 ml) water in large slow cooker.

- Cover and cook on low for 6 to 8 hours.

- Turn heat to high, add stewed tomatoes and green beans and stir well.

- Continue cooking for an additional 30 minutes or until green beans are tender. Serves 6 to 8.

TIP: Serve with toasted focaccia.

Ham, Bean and Pasta Soup

1 onion, finely chopped
2 sticks celery, chopped
2 teaspoons minced garlic
1 litre carton chicken stock
2 425-g (15-ounce) cans chilli
   with liquid
3 cups (420 g) cooked, cubed ham
⅓ cup (35 g) pasta shells
Bacon, cooked

- Combine onion, celery, garlic, chicken stock, beans, ham and 1 cup (250 ml) water in 5 to 6-L (5 to 6-quart) slow cooker.

- Cover and cook on low for 4 to 5 hours.

- Turn cooker to high heat, add pasta shells and cook for additional 35 to 45 minutes or until pasta is tender.

- Garnish each serving with cooked, crisp and crumbled bacon. Serves 6 to 8.

French Onion Soup

5–6 onions, thinly sliced
1 clove garlic, minced
2 tablespoons (30 g) butter
1 litre carton beef stock
2 teaspoons Worcestershire sauce
6–8 2.5-cm (1-inch) slices white
**   bread**
8 slices Swiss cheese

- Cook onions and garlic in large frypan on low heat (DO NOT BROWN) in hot butter for about 20 minutes and stir several times.

- Transfer onion mixture to 4 to 5-L (4 to 5-quart) slow cooker. Add beef stock, Worcestershire sauce and 1 cup (250 ml) water.

- Cover and cook on low for 5 to 8 hours or on high for 2 hours 30 minutes to 4 hours.

- Before serving soup, toast bread slices with cheese slice on top. Grill for 3 to 4 minutes or until cheese is light brown and bubbly.

- Ladle soup into bowls and top with toast. Serves 6 to 8.

Tortellini Soup

30 g (1 ounce) white sauce mix
3 boneless, skinless chicken
**   breast halves**
½ litre carton chicken stock
1 teaspoon minced garlic
½ teaspoon dried basil
½ teaspoon oregano
½ teaspoon cayenne pepper
230 g (8 ounces) cheese-filled
**   tortellini**
1½ cups (375 ml) unthickened
**   cream**
6 cups (180 g) fresh baby spinach

- Place white sauce mix in sprayed 5 to 6-L (5 to 6-quart) slow cooker.

- Stir in 4 cups (1 L) water and stir gradually until mixture is smooth.

- Cut chicken into 2.5-cm (1-inch) pieces. Add chicken, stock, garlic, basil, oregano, cayenne pepper and ½ teaspoon (2 ml) salt to mixture.

- Cover and cook on low for 6 to 7 hours or on high for 3 hours.

- Stir in pasta, cover and cook for additional 1 hour on high.

- Stir in cream and fresh spinach and cook just enough for soup to get hot. Serves 4 to 6.

TIP: Sprinkle a little shredded parmesan cheese on top of each serving.

Enchilada Soup

**455 g (1 pound) lean minced
  beef, browned, drained
1 425-g (15-ounce) can
  stewed tomatoes
1 425-g (15-ounce) can borlotti
  beans with liquid
1 425-g (15-ounce) can corn
  kernels with liquid
1 onion, chopped
2 280-g (10-ounce) cans
  enchilada sauce
230 g (8 ounces) shredded cheese
Corn chips**

- Combine beef, tomatoes, beans, corn, onion, enchilada sauce and 1 cup (250 ml) water in sprayed 5 to 6-L (5 to 6-quart) slow cooker and mix well.

- Cover and cook on low for 6 to 8 hours or on high for 3 to 4 hours.

- Stir in shredded cheese.

- If desired, top each serving with a few crushed corn chips. Serves 6 to 8.

Hamburger Soup

910 g (2 pounds) lean minced
  beef
2 425-g (15-ounce) jars chunky
  vegetable pasta sauce
455 g (16 ounces) frozen mixed
  vegetables, thawed
1 litre carton beef stock
2 425-g (15-ounce) cans stewed
  tomatoes
1 teaspoon seasoned salt

- Brown beef in frypan until no
  longer pink.

- Place in 6-L (6-quart) slow
  cooker.

- Add pasta sauce, vegetables,
  stock, tomatoes, 1 cup (250 ml)
  water and seasoned salt and stir
  well.

- Cover and cook on low for
  6 to 7 hours. Serves 6 to 8.

Tasty Lentil Soup

455 g (1 pound) hot sausage meat
1 onion, chopped
1 litre carton chicken stock
2 425-g (15-ounce) cans
  stewed tomatoes
1 green capsicum, seeded,
  chopped
2 425-g (15-ounce) cans lentils,
  rinsed, drained

- Break up sausage and brown
  with onion in large frypan. Drain
  off fat and place in large slow
  cooker.

- Add chicken stock, stewed
  tomatoes, capsicum, lentils and
  1 cup (250 ml) water. Cover and
  cook on low for 3 to 5 hours.
  Serves 4 to 6.

Sausage-Pizza Soup

455 g (16 ounces) Italian
  sausages, thinly sliced
1 onion, chopped
2 115-g (4-ounce) cans sliced
  mushrooms
1 small green capsicum, cored,
  seeded, julienned
1 425-g (15-ounce) can Italian
  stewed tomatoes
½ litre (14 ounces) carton beef
  stock
1 230-g (8-ounce) can pizza sauce
Shredded mozzarella cheese

- Combine all ingredients except
  cheese in slow cooker and stir
  well.

- Cover and cook on low for
  4 to 5 hours.

- Sprinkle mozzarella cheese over
  each serving. Serves 4 to 6.

Turkey and Mushroom Soup

*Another great way to use
leftover chicken or turkey.*

2 cups (145 g) sliced shitake
  mushrooms
2 sticks celery, sliced
1 small onion, chopped
2 tablespoons (30 g) butter
1 425-g (15-ounce) can
  sliced carrots
1 litre carton chicken stock
½ cup (40 g) orzo pasta
2 cups (280 g) cooked, chopped
  turkey

- Sauté mushrooms, celery and
  onion in butter in frypan.

- Transfer vegetables to slow
  cooker and add carrots, stock,
  pasta and turkey. (Do not use
  smoked turkey.)

- Cover and cook on low for
  2 to 3 hours or on high for
  1 to 2 hours. Serves 4 to 6.

Creamy Vegetable Soup

1½ litres chicken stock
¼ cup (60 g) butter, melted
455 g (16 ounces) frozen mixed
    vegetables
1 onion, chopped
3 sticks celery, sliced
1 teaspoon ground cumin
3 zucchini, coarsely chopped
2 cups (480 ml) chopped, fresh
    broccoli florets
1 cup (250 ml) unthickened
    cream

- Combine stock, butter, vegetables, onion, celery, cumin, 1 teaspoon (5 ml) each of salt and pepper in large slow cooker and stir well.

- Cover and cook on low for 6 to 7 hours or on high for 3 to 4 hours.

- Stir in zucchini and broccoli. If not using high temperature, turn heat to high and cook an additional 30 minutes to 1 hour or until broccoli is tender but crisp.

- Turn off heat and stir in cream. Let stand for 10 minutes before serving. Serves 6 to 8.

Cream of Zucchini Soup

1 small onion, very finely
    chopped
3½–4 cups (440–500 g) grated
    zucchini with peels
1 litre carton chicken stock
1 teaspoon seasoned salt
1 teaspoon dried dill
½ teaspoon white pepper
2 tablespoons (30 g) butter,
    melted
230 g (8 ounces) sour cream

- Combine all ingredients except sour cream in small, sprayed slow cooker.

- Cover and cook on low for 2 hours.

- Fold in sour cream and continue cooking for about 10 minutes or just until soup is hot. Serves 4.

Lentil Soup

1 litre carton chicken stock
3 425-g (15-ounce) cans lentils
rinsed, drained
2 280-g (10-ounces) cans
tomatoes
2 green chillies, chopped
1 onion, chopped
1 teaspoon ground cumin
½ teaspoon dried thyme
½ teaspoon dried oregano
2–3 cups (280–420 g) cooked,
finely diced ham

- Combine chicken stock and lentils in slow cooker and turn cooker to high.

- Cook just long enough for ingredients to get hot.

- Mash about half of lentils in cooker.

- Reduce heat to low and add tomatoes, green chillies, onion, cumin, thyme, oregano, ham and ¾ cup (175 ml) water.

- Cover and cook for 5 to 6 hours. Serves 6 to 8.

Confetti-Chicken Soup

455 g (1 pound) boneless, skinless chicken thighs
170 g (6 ounces) chicken flavoured rice
1½ litres chicken stock
3 carrots, sliced
1 280-g (10-ounce) can cream of chicken soup
1½ tablespoons (22 ml) chicken seasoning
280 g (10 ounces) frozen corn kernels, thawed
280 g (10 ounces) frozen baby green peas, thawed

- Cut thighs in thin strips.

- Combine chicken, rice, chicken stock, carrots, soup, seasoning and 1 cup (250 ml) water in 5 to 6-L (5 to 6-quart) slow cooker.

- Cover and cook on low for 8 to 9 hours.

- About 30 minutes before serving, turn heat to high and add corn and peas to cooker. Continue cooking for an additional 30 minutes. Serves 4 to 6.

Tasty Cabbage and Beef Soup

455 g (1 pound) lean minced beef
1 cup shredded red cabbage
1 cup shredded green cabbage
1 cup shredded carrot
1 425-g (15-ounce) can cut green beans
1 425-g (15-ounce) can corn kernels
2 425-g (15-ounce) cans Italian stewed tomatoes
1 litre carton beef stock
Cornbread

- Brown beef in frypan, drain fat and place in large slow cooker.

- Add carrot, cabbages, green beans, corn, tomatoes and beef stock and add a little salt and pepper.

- Cover and cook on low for 7 to 9 hours. Serve with cornbread. Serves 6 to 8.

Chilli Soup

3 425-g (15-ounce) cans chilli with beans
1 425-g (15-ounce) can corn kernels
½ litre carton beef stock
2 425-g (15-ounce) cans stewed tomatoes
2 teaspoons ground cumin
2 teaspoons chilli powder
Flour tortillas

- Combine chilli, corn, stock, tomatoes, cumin, chilli powder and 1 cup (250 ml) water in 5 to 6-L (5 to 6-quart) slow cooker.

- Cover and cook on low for 4 to 5 hours. Serve with warm, buttered flour tortillas. Serves 6 to 8.

Chicken and Rice Soup

170 g (6 ounces) long grain wild
   rice mix
30 g (1 ounce) chicken noodle
   soup mix
2 280-g (10-ounce) cans cream of
   chicken soup
2 sticks celery, chopped
1–2 cups (140–280 g) cooked,
   cubed chicken

- Combine rice mix, noodle soup
  mix, chicken soup, celery,
  chicken and about 6 cups (1.4 L)
  water in 5 to 6-L (5 to 6-quart)
  slow cooker.

- Cover and cook on low for
  2 to 3 hours. Serves 4 to 6.

Chicken and Barley Soup

680–910 g (1½–2 pounds)
   boneless, skinless chicken
   thighs
455 g (16 ounces) frozen stew
   vegetables
30 g (1 ounce) vegetable soup
   mix
1¼ cups (250 g) pearl barley
1 litre carton chicken
1 teaspoon white pepper

- Combine all ingredients with
  1 teaspoon salt and 4 cups
  (1 L) water in large, sprayed
  slow cooker.

- Cover and cook on low for
  5 to 6 hours or on high for
  3 hours. Serves 6 to 8.

Chicken-Pasta Soup

680 g (1½ pounds) boneless,
  skinless chicken thighs, cubed
1 onion, chopped
3 carrots, sliced
½ cup (65 g) halved, pitted
  black olives
1 teaspoon minced garlic
1½ litres chicken stock
1 425-g (15-ounce) can Italian
  stewed tomatoes
1 teaspoon Italian seasoning
½ cup (55 g) small pasta shells
Parmesan cheese

- Combine all ingredients except pasta shells and parmesan cheese in slow cooker.

- Cover and cook on low for 8 to 9 hours. About 30 minutes before serving, add pasta and stir.

- Increase heat to high and cook for additional 20 to 30 minutes. Garnish with parmesan cheese. Serves 6 to 8.

Vegetable-Lentil Soup

2 540-g (19-ounce) cans lentil
    home-style soup
1 425-g (15-ounce) can
    stewed tomatoes
½ litre carton chicken stock
1 onion, chopped
1 green capsicum, chopped
3 sticks celery, sliced
1 carrot, halved lengthwise,
    sliced
2 teaspoons minced garlic
1 teaspoon dried marjoram
    leaves

- Combine all ingredients in slow
  cooker and stir well.

- Cover and cook on low for
  5 to 6 hours. Serves 6 to 8.

Cheesy Potato Soup

6 medium potatoes, peeled, cubed
1 onion, very finely chopped
1 litre carton chicken stock
½ teaspoon white pepper
230 g (8 ounces) shredded
    cheddar cheese
1 cup (250 ml) cream

- Combine potatoes, onion,
  chicken stock and white pepper
  in slow cooker.

- Cover and cook on low for
  8 to 10 hours. Mash potatoes in
  slow cooker.

- About 1 hour before serving, stir
  in cheese and cream and cook an
  additional 1 hour. Serves 4 to 6.

Turkey-Tortilla Soup

This is great for leftover turkey.

1 litre carton chicken stock
2 425-g (15-ounce) cans stewed
   tomatoes
210 g (7 ounces) butter beans
210 g (7 ounces) corn kernels
2 teaspoons chilli powder
1 teaspoon dried coriander
2 cups (110 g) crushed corn chips
2½ cups (350 g) cooked, chopped
   turkey

- Combine stock, tomatoes, beans, corn, chilli powder, coriander, ⅓ cup (19 g) crushed corn chips and turkey in large slow cooker and stir well.

- Cover and cook on low for 3 to 5 hours.

- When ready to serve, sprinkle remaining chips over each serving. Serves 6 to 8.

TIP: Do not use smoked turkey.

Cheddar Soup Plus

2 cups (500 ml) milk
1 200-g (15-ounce) can cream of
    asparagus condensed soup
1 cup (140 g) cooked, finely
    chopped chicken breasts
280 g (10 ounces) frozen green
    peas, thawed
Shredded cheddar cheese

- Place 4 cups (1 L) water and
  milk in slow cooker. Set heat on
  high until water and milk come
  to the boil.

- Stir contents of soup into hot
  water and milk and stir well.
  Add chopped chicken, green
  peas and a little salt and pepper.

- Cover and cook on low for
  2 to 3 hours.

- To serve, sprinkle cheddar
  cheese over each serving of
  soup. Serves 4.

Cajun Bean Soup

570 g (20 ounces) Italian-style
    soup mix
4 teaspoons Cajun seasoning
2 cups (280 g) cooked, finely
    chopped ham
1 chopped onion
2 425-g (15-ounce) cans stewed
    tomatoes
Cornbread

- Soak soup mix overnight in
  large slow cooker. After soaking,
  drain water and cover with
  2 inches water over soup mix.

- Cover and cook on low for
  5 to 6 hours or until legumes
  are tender.

- Add ham, onion, stewed
  tomatoes and seasoning in soup
  mix.

- Cover and cook on high for
  30 to 45 minutes.

- Serve with cornbread.
  Serves 4 to 6.

Black-Eyed Soup

5 slices thick-cut bacon, diced
1 onion, chopped
1 green capsicum, chopped
3 sticks celery, sliced
2 cups black-eyed peas
2 425-g (15-ounce) cans stewed
   tomatoes with liquid
1 teaspoon chicken seasoning

- Cook bacon pieces in frypan until crisp, drain on paper towel and place in slow cooker.

- With bacon drippings in frypan, sauté onion and capsicum, but do not brown.

- Add onions, capsicum, celery, black-eyed peas, stewed tomatoes, 2½ cups (600 ml) water and chicken seasoning to slow cooker.

- Cover and cook on low for 3 to 4 hours. Serves 6 to 8.

Beefy Rice Soup

455 g (1 pound) lean beef
   stew meat
½ litre carton beef stock
200 g (7 ounces) beef-flavoured
   rice
280 g (10 ounces) frozen peas and
   carrots
2½ cups (625 ml) vegetable juice

- Sprinkle stew meat with seasoned pepper, brown in non-stick frypan, drain and place in large slow cooker.

- Add stock, rice, peas and carrots, vegetable juice and 2 cups (500 ml) water.

- Cover and cook on low for 6 to 7 hours. Serves 4 to 6.

Beef and Lentil Soup

455 g (1 pound) lean minced beef
2 onions, chopped
2 cups (480 ml) sliced celery
1 litre carton beef stock
1 425-g (15-ounce) can stewed tomatoes
1 teaspoon chilli powder
2 425-g (15-ounce) cans lentils, rinsed, drained

- Brown beef in frypan until no longer pink. Place in 5 to 6-L (5 to 6-quart) slow cooker.

- Add onions, celery, stock, tomatoes, lentils, ¾ cup (175 ml) water plus a little salt and pepper.

- Cover and cook on low for 6 to 7 hours or on high for 3 hours to 3 hours 30 minutes. Serves 6 to 8.

TIP: If you like a zestier soup, add more chilli powder.

Beef and Pasta Soup

**680 g (1½ pounds) lean
  minced beef
1 onion, chopped
2 425-g (15-ounce) cans mixed
  vegetables, drained
2 425-g (15-ounce) cans
  Italian stewed tomatoes
1 litre carton beef stock
1 teaspoon dried oregano
1 cup (75 g) fettuccini
  (medium egg noodles)**

- Brown and cook beef in frypan until no longer pink and transfer to slow cooker.

- Add onion, mixed vegetables, stewed tomatoes, beef stock and oregano.

- Cover and cook on low for 4 to 5 hours.

- Cook pasta according to package direction.

- Add pasta to slow cooker and cook for an additional 30 minutes. Serves 4 to 6.

Beef and Barley Soup

455 g (1 pound) lean minced beef
1½ litres beef stock
¾ cup (150 g) quick-cooking barley
3 cups (365 g) sliced carrots
2 cups (200 g) sliced celery
2 teaspoons steak seasoning

- Brown beef in frypan, drain and transfer to 5-L (5-quart) slow cooker.

- Add beef stock, barley, carrots, celery and steak seasoning. Cover and cook on low for 7 to 8 hours. Serves 4.

Beans and Barley Soup

2 425-g (15-ounce) cans borlotti beans with liquid
1½ litres chicken stock
½ cup (100 g) quick-cooking barley
1 425-g (15-ounce) can Italian stewed tomatoes

- Combine beans, stock, barley, stewed tomatoes and ½ teaspoon pepper in 6-L (6-quart) slow cooker and stir well.

- Cover and cook on low for 4 to 5 hours. Serves 6 to 8.

Beans 'n Sausage Soup

455 g (1 pound) hot Italian
    sausages
1 onion, chopped
1 425-g (15-ounce) can Italian
    stewed tomatoes
2 145-g (5-ounce) cans
    red kidney beans,
    rinsed, drained
2 425-g (15-ounce) cans
    cannellini beans with
    liquid
1 litre carton beef stock
1 teaspoon minced garlic
1 teaspoon dried basil

- Cut sausages into 1.2-cm (½-inch) pieces. Brown sausages and onion in frypan, drain and transfer to 5 to 6-L (5 to 6-quart) slow cooker.

- Stir in tomatoes, kidney beans, cannellini beans, stock, garlic and basil and mix well. Cover and cook on low for 5 to 7 hours. Serves 6 to 8.

Minestrone Soup

2 425-g (15-ounce) cans
    Italian stewed tomatoes
2 455-g (16-ounce) frozen
    vegetables
2 cups spiral pasta, cooked,
    drained
1½ litres beef stock
2 sticks celery, chopped
2 potatoes, peeled, cubed
1 teaspoon Italian herb
    seasoning
2 425-g (15-ounce) cans
    kidney beans, drained,
    rinsed
2 teaspoons minced garlic

- Combine tomatoes, vegetables,
  cooked pasta stock, celery,
  potatoes, seasoning, beans,
  garlic and 1 cup (250 ml) water
  in large, sprayed slow cooker
  and mix well.

- Cover and cook on low for
  4 to 6 hours. Serves 8 to 10.

Chicken-Tortellini Stew

255 g (9 ounces) package
    refrigerated cheese-filled
    tortellini
2 medium yellow squash,
    halved, sliced
1 red capsicum, seeded, coarsely
    chopped
1 onion, chopped
1 litre carton chicken stock
1 teaspoon dried rosemary
½ teaspoon dried basil
2 cups (280 g) cooked,
    chopped chicken

- Place pasta, squash, capsicum
  and onion in slow cooker. Stir
  in stock, rosemary, basil and
  chicken.

- Cover and cook on low for
  2 to 4 hours or until pasta and
  vegetables are tender. Serves 4.

Winter Minestrone

455 g (1 pound) Italian sausages
2 medium potatoes, peeled
2 medium fennel bulbs,
    trimmed
2½ cups (285 g) butternut
    pumpkin
1 onion, chopped
1 425-g (15-ounce) can kidney
    beans, rinsed, drained
2 teaspoons minced garlic
1 teaspoon Italian seasoning
1 litre carton chicken stock
1 cup (250 ml) dry white wine
3–4 cups (90–120 g) fresh
    spinach

- Cut sausages, potatoes and fennel into 1.2-cm (½-inch) slices.

- Cook sausages in frypan until brown and drain.

- Combine squash, potatoes, fennel, onion, beans, garlic and Italian seasoning in large slow cooker.

- Top with sausage and pour chicken stock and wine over all.

- Cover and cook on low for 7 to 9 hours.

- Stir in spinach, cover and cook for an additional 10 minutes. Serves 6 to 8.

Pancho Villa Stew

3 cups (420 g) cooked,
**   diced ham**
455 g (1 pound) smoked
**   sausages**
1½ litres chicken stock
1 425-g (15-ounce) can
**   diced tomatoes**
3 green chillies, chopped
1 onion, chopped
2 425-g (15-ounce) cans
**   borlotti beans with liquid**
1 425-g (15-ounce) can
**   corn kernels**
1 teaspoon garlic powder
2 teaspoons ground cumin
2 teaspoons cocoa
1 teaspoon dried oregano
Flour tortillas

- Cut sausages into 1.2-cm (½-inch) pieces.

- Combine all ingredients and 1 teaspoon salt except tortillas in slow cooker and stir well.

- Cover and cook on low for 5 to 7 hours.

- Serve with buttered, flour tortillas. Serves 6 to 8.

A Different Stew

**910 g (2 pounds) premium lean
  beef stew meat**
**455 g (16 ounces) frozen
  Cantonese stir-fry
  vegetables, thawed**
**1 280-g (10-ounce) can
  mushroom soup**
½ litre carton beef stock
**⅔ cup (150 ml) bottled
  sweet-and-sour sauce**
**1 tablespoon (15 ml) steak
  seasoning**

- Brown stew meat sprinkled with ½ teaspoon black pepper in frypan and place in slow cooker.

- Combine vegetables, soup, stock, sweet-and-sour sauce, steak seasoning and 1 cup (250 ml) water in bowl. Pour over stew meat and stir well.

- Cover and cook on low for 5 to 7 hours. Serves 4 to 6.

Chicken Stew

**4 large boneless, skinless
  chicken breast halves,
  cubed**
**3 medium potatoes, peeled,
  cubed**
**1 740-g (26-ounce) jar meatless
  spaghetti sauce**
**1 425-g (15-ounce) can cut
  green beans, drained**
**1 425-g (15-ounce) can
  corn kernels**
**1 tablespoon (15 ml) chicken
  seasoning**

- Combine chicken, potatoes, spaghetti sauce, green beans, corn, chicken seasoning and ¾ cup (175 ml) water in 5 to 6-L (5 to 6-quart) slow cooker.

- Cover and cook on low for 6 to 7 hours. Serves 4 to 6.

Southern Ham Stew

This is great served with cornbread.

2 cups (480 g) dried
   black-eyed peas
3 cups (420 g) cooked, cubed ham
1 large onion, chopped
2 cups (200 g) sliced celery
1 425-g (15-ounce) can
   cannellini beans, drained
2 425-g (15-ounce) cans
   stewed tomatoes
1½ cups chicken stock
2 teaspoons seasoned salt
2 tablespoons cornflour

- Rinse and drain dried black-eyed peas in saucepan. Cover peas with water, bring to a boil and drain again.

- Place peas in large slow cooker and add 5 cups (1.2 L) water, ham, onion, celery, cannellini beans, tomatoes, stock and seasoned salt.

- Cover and cook on low for 7 to 9 hours. Mix cornflour with ⅓ cup (75 ml) water in bowl, turn cooker to high heat, pour in cornflour mixture and stir well.

- Cook for about 10 minutes or until stew thickens.
  Serves 6 to 8.

TIP: If you would like a little spice in the stew, add a teaspoon of chilli powder.

Serious Bean Stew

455 g (16 ounces) smoked
   sausages
1 795-g (28-ounce) can baked
   beans with liquid
1 425-g (15-ounce) can
   cannellini beans with liquid
1 425-g (15-ounce) can borlotti
   beans with liquid
1 425-g (15-ounce) can lentils
1 onion, chopped
1 teaspoon Cajun seasoning
2 425-g (15-ounce) cans stewed
   tomatoes
Muffins

- Peel skin from sausages and slice.

- Place in 6-L (6-quart) slow cooker, add remaining ingredients and stir to mix.

- Cover and cook on low for 3 to 4 hours.

- Serve with muffins. Serves 6 to 8.

Santa Fe Stew

A hearty, filling soup.

**680 g (1½ pounds) lean
    minced beef**
½ litre carton beef stock
**1 425-g (15-ounce) can corn
    kernels with liquid**
**2 425-g (15-ounce) cans
    borlotti beans with liquid**
**2 425-g (15-ounce) cans
    stewed tomatoes**
2 teaspoons chilli powder
1 teaspoon steak seasoning
**455 g (16 ounces) cubed
    cheddar cheese**

- Brown beef in frypan until no longer pink.

- Place in 5 to 6-L (5 to 6-quart) slow cooker and add stock, corn, beans, tomatoes, chilli powder and steak seasoning.

- Cover and cook on low for 5 to 6 hours.

- When ready to serve, fold in cheese and stir until cheese melts. Serves 6 to 8.

TIP: Cornbread is a must to serve with this stew.

Pork-Vegetable Stew

910 g (2 pounds) pork tenderloin
1 onion, coarsely chopped
1 red capsicum, julienned
455 g (16 ounces) frozen mixed
    vegetables, thawed
2 tablespoons (15 g) flour
½ teaspoon dried rosemary
    leaves
½ teaspoon oregano leaves
1½ cups chicken stock
170 g (6 ounces) long
    grain wild rice

- Cut pork into 2.5-cm (1-inch) cubes. Brown pork cubes in non-stick frypan and place in large, sprayed slow cooker.

- Add onion, capsicum and mixed vegetables.

- Combine flour, rosemary and oregano into chicken stock in bowl and pour over vegetables.

- Cover and cook on low for 4 hours to 4 hours 30 minutes.

- When ready to serve, cook rice according to package directions.

- Serve pork and vegetables over rice. Serves 4 to 6.

Roast and Vegetable Stew

3 cups (420 g) leftover roast
   beef, cubed
2 425-g (15-ounce) cans
   stewed tomatoes
455 g (16 ounces) frozen mixed
   vegetables, thawed
1 litre carton beef stock
1 cup (100 g) cauliflower
   florets
1 cup (70 g) broccoli florets

- Combine all ingredients except cauliflower and broccoli in 6-L (6-quart) slow cooker. Add a little salt and pepper.

- Cover and cook on low for 3 to 4 hours.

- Stir in cauliflower and broccoli and continue cooking for an additional 2 hours until tender. Serves 6 to 8.

Olé! For Stew

680–910 g (1½–2 pounds) lean
   beef stew meat
2 425-g (15-ounce) cans
   borlotti beans with liquid
1 onion, chopped
3 carrots, sliced
2 medium potatoes, cubed
30 g (1 ounce)
   taco seasoning
2 425-g (15-ounce) cans
   stewed tomatoes
2 teaspoons chilli powder
Flour tortillas

- Brown stew meat in non-stick frypan. Combine meat, borlotti beans, onion, carrots, potatoes, taco seasoning and 2 cups (500 ml) water in large slow cooker.

- Cover and cook on low for 6 to 7 hours. Add stewed tomatoes and cook for an additional 1 hour. Serves 4 to 6.

TIP: This is great served with warmed, buttered, flour tortillas.

Meatball Stew

510 g (18 ounces) frozen
    prepared meatballs,
    thawed
½ litre carton beef stock
1 425-g (15-ounce) can cut
    green beans
455 g (16 ounces) baby carrots
2 425-g (15-ounce) cans stewed
    tomatoes
1 tablespoon (15 ml)
    Worcestershire sauce
½ teaspoon ground allspice

- Combine all ingredients in
  slow cooker.

- Cover and cook on low for
  3 to 5 hours. Serves 4 to 6.

Meatball and Veggie Stew

510 g (18 ounces) frozen cooked
    meatballs, thawed
455 g (16 ounces) frozen mixed
    vegetables
1 425-g (15-ounce) can stewed
    tomatoes
340 g (12 ounces) carton beef
    gravy
2 teaspoons crushed
    dried basil

- Place meatballs and mixed
  vegetables in 4 to 5-L
  (4 to 5-quart) slow cooker.

- Combine stewed tomatoes,
  gravy, basil, ½ teaspoon black
  pepper and ½ cup
  (125 ml) water in bowl. Pour
  over meatballs and vegetables.

- Cover and cook on low for
  6 to 7 hours. Serves 4 to 6.

Italian-Vegetable Stew

680–910 g (1½–2 pounds) Italian
   sausage meat
910 g (32 ounces) frozen
   vegetables
2 425-g (15-ounce) cans
   Italian stewed tomatoes
½ litre carton beef stock
1 teaspoon Italian seasoning
½ cup (55 g) pasta shells

- Brown sausage meat and cook in frypan for about 5 minutes and drain.

- Combine sausage, vegetables, stewed tomatoes, stock, Italian seasoning and pasta shells in 5 to 6-L (5 to 6-quart) slow cooker and mix well.

- Cover and cook on low for 3 to 5 hours. Serves 4 to 6.

Hungarian Stew

910 g (2 pounds) boneless
   short ribs
1 cup (200 g) pearl barley
1 small onion, chopped
1 green capsicum, cored,
   seeded, chopped
1 teaspoon minced garlic
2 425-g (15-ounce) cans
   kidney beans, drained
1 litre carton beef stock
1 tablespoon (15 ml) paprika

- Combine all ingredients plus 1 cup (250 ml) water in slow cooker.

- Cover and cook on low for 8 to 9 hours or on high for 4 hours 30 minutes to 5 hours. Serves 4 to 6.

Hearty Meatball Stew

795 g (28 ounces) frozen
    meatballs, thawed
2 425-g (15-ounce) cans Italian
    stewed tomatoes
1 litre carton beef stock
2 425-g (15-ounce) cans
    new potatoes
455 g (16 ounces) baby carrots
1 tablespoon (15 ml) steak
    seasoning
Muffins

- Place meatballs, stewed tomatoes, beef stock, potatoes, carrots and steak seasoning in 6-L (6-quart) slow cooker.

- Cover and cook on low for 6 to 7 hours.

- Serve with muffins. Serves 6 to 8.

Ham and Cabbage Stew

2 425-g (15-ounce) cans Italian
    stewed tomatoes
3 cups (210 g) shredded cabbage
1 onion, chopped
1 red capsicum, cored,
    seeded, chopped
2 tablespoons (30 g) butter,
    sliced
½ litre carton
    chicken stock
¾ teaspoon seasoned salt
3 cups (420 g) cooked,
    diced ham
Cornbread

- Combine all ingredients with ¾ teaspoon pepper and 1 cup (250 ml) water in large slow cooker and stir to mix well.

- Cover and cook on low for 5 to 7 hours.

- Serve with cornbread. Serves 4 to 6.

South-of-the-Border Beef Stew

**680–910 g (1½–2 pounds)
  boneless, beef chuck roast**
1 green capsicum
2 onions, coarsely chopped
**2 425-g (15-ounce) cans borlotti
  beans with liquid**
½ cup (95 g) rice
½ litre carton beef stock
**2 425-g (15-ounce) cans
  stewed tomatoes**
**1 cup (265 g) mild or medium
  green salsa**
2 teaspoons ground cumin
Flour tortillas

- Trim fat from beef and cut into 2.5-cm (1-inch) cubes.

- Brown beef in large frypan and place in large, sprayed slow cooker.

- Cut capsicum into 1.2-cm (½-inch) slices.

- Add remaining ingredients plus 1½ cups (375 ml) water and a little salt.

- Cover and cook on low for 7 to 8 hours.

- Serve with warm, flour tortillas. Serves 6 to 8.

Comfort Stew

680 g (1½ pounds) select stew meat
2 280-g (10-ounce) cans French onion soup
1 280-g (10-ounce) can cream of onion soup
1 280-g (10-ounce) can cream of celery soup
455 g (16 ounces) package frozen stew vegetables, thawed

- Place stew meat in sprayed slow cooker.

- Add soups as listed and spread evenly over meat. Do not stir.

- Turn slow cooker to high and cook just long enough for ingredients to get hot.

- Change heat setting to low, cover and cook for 6 to 7 hours. Add vegetables and continue cooking for additional 1 hour. Serves 4 to 6.

Chicken Stew over Rice

**60 g (2 ounces) chicken
    gravy mix
2 cups (200 g) sliced celery
280 g (10 ounces) frozen sliced
    carrots
280 g (10 ounces) frozen green
    peas, thawed
1 teaspoon dried basil
3 cups (280 g) cubed cooked
    chicken
Steamed white rice**

- Combine gravy mix, 2 cups (500 ml) water, celery, carrots, peas, basil, ¾ teaspoon each of salt and pepper and chicken in slow cooker.

- Cover and cook on low for 6 to 7 hours. Serve over steamed white rice. Serves 4 to 6.

TIP: If you like thick stew, mix 2 tablespoons (15 g) cornflour with ¼ cup (60 ml) water and stir into chicken mixture. Cook an additional 30 minutes to thicken.

White Lightning Chilli

3 425-g (15-ounce) cans
cannellini beans with
liquid
1½ litres chicken stock
280-g (10-ounce) can cream of
chicken soup
2 tablespoons (28 g) butter,
melted
2 onions, chopped
3 cups (420 g) cooked, chopped
chicken or turkey
2 green chillies, chopped
1 teaspoon minced garlic
½ teaspoon dried basil
½ teaspoon white pepper
⅛ teaspoon cayenne pepper
⅛ teaspoon ground cloves
1 teaspoon ground oregano
230 g (8 ounces) shredded
cheddar cheese

- Combine all ingredients except
cheese in slow cooker.

- Cover and cook on low for
4 to 5 hours.

- When serving, sprinkle cheese
over top of each serving.
Serves 6 to 8.

Vegetarian Chilli

**2 425-g (15-ounce) cans
  stewed tomatoes
1 425-g (15-ounce) can kidney
  beans, rinsed, drained
1 425-g (15-ounce) can borlotti
  beans with liquid
1 onion, chopped
1 green capsicum, seeded,
  chopped
1 tablespoon (15 ml) chilli
  powder
200 g (7 ounces) elbow macaroni
¼ cup (60 g) butter, melted**

- Combine tomatoes, kidney beans, borlotti beans, onion, capsicum, chilli powder and 1 cup (250 ml) water in 4 to 5-L (4 to 5-quart) slow cooker.

- Cover and cook on low for 4 to 5 hours or on high for 2 hours.

- Cook pasta according to package directions, drain and stir in melted butter. Fold pasta into chilli.

- If desired, top each serving with shredded cheddar cheese. Serves 4 to 6.

Vegetable Chilli

2 425-g (15-ounce) cans
     cannellini beans with liquid
1 425-g (15-ounce) can borlotti
     beans with liquid
2 425-g (15-ounce) cans stewed
     tomatoes
1 425-g (15-ounce) can
     corn kernels
1 onion, chopped
3 sticks celery, sliced
1 tablespoon (15 ml) chilli
     powder
2 teaspoons dried oregano leaves
1 teaspoon seasoned salt
Cornbread

- In 5-L (5 to 6-quart) slow cooker, combine beans, tomatoes, corn, onion, celery, chilli powder, oregano, seasoned salt and 1½ cups (375 ml) water.

- Cover and cook on low for 4 to 6 hours.

- Serve with hot, buttered cornbread. Serves 6 to 8.

Traditional Chilli

910 g (2 pounds) lean minced
  beef
1 large onion, finely chopped
1 280-g (10-ounce) can chopped
  tomatoes
2 green chillies, chopped
2½ cups (625 ml) tomato juice
2 tablespoons (15 g) chilli
  powder
1 tablespoon (15 ml) ground
  cumin
1 tablespoon (15 ml) minced
  garlic
1 425-g (15-ounce) can borlotti
  or kidney beans

- Combine beef, onion, tomatoes, green chillies, tomato juice, chilli powder, cumin, garlic and 1 cup (250 ml) water in large slow cooker and mix well.

- Cover and cook on low for 7 to 9 hours.

- Add borlotti or kidney beans and continue to cook for an additional 30 minutes. Serves 4 to 6.

Turkey-Veggie Chilli

455 g (1 pound) minced turkey
Canola oil
2 425-g (15-ounce) cans
    borlotti beans with liquid
1 425-g (15-ounce) can cannellini
    beans with liquid
½ litre carton chicken stock
2 425-g (15-ounce) cans
    stewed tomatoes
1 230-g (8-ounce) can
    corn kernels
1 large onion, chopped
1 red capsicum, chopped
2 teaspoons minced garlic
2 teaspoons ground cumin
½ cup (55 g) elbow macaroni

- Cook and brown turkey in frypan with a little oil before placing in large slow cooker.

- Add beans, stock, tomatoes, corn, onion, capsicum, garlic, cumin and a little salt and stir well.

- Cover and cook on low for 4 to 5 hours.

- Stir in pasta and continue cooking for about 15 minutes or until macaroni is tender. Serves 6 to 8.

TIP: Top each serving with dab of sour cream or 1 tablespoon (15 ml) shredded cheddar cheese.

Easy Chilli

**1.8 kg (4 pounds) lean
minced beef
560 g (20 ounces) packages
hot chilli mix
1 170-g (6-ounce) can
tomato soup
2 425-g (15-ounce) cans stewed
tomatoes with liquid
2½ teaspoons ground cumin**

• Break beef into pieces and
brown in large frypan
and drain. Use slotted spoon
to drain fat and place beef in
5 to 6-L (5 to 6-quart)
slow cooker.

• Add chilli mix, tomato soup,
stewed tomatoes, cumin,
1 teaspoon salt and 1 cup
(250 ml) water.

• Cover and cook on low for
4 to 5 hours. Serves 6 to 8.

*TIP: If you think you can't eat
chilli without beans, add
2 (15 ounce/425 g) cans
chilli beans.*

Chunky Chilli

910 g (2 pounds) premium
    cut stew meat
1 onion, chopped
2 425-g (15-ounce) cans
    diced tomatoes
2 425-g (15-ounce) cans
    borlotti beans with
    liquid
1½ tablespoons (22 ml) chilli
    powder
2 teaspoons ground cumin
1 teaspoon ground oregano
Shredded cheddar cheese

- If stew meat is in fairly large chunks, cut each chunk in half.

- Brown stew meat in large frypan and transfer to large slow cooker.

- Add onion, tomatoes, beans, chilli powder, cumin, oregano and a little salt.

- Cover and cook on low for 6 to 7 hours.

- Sprinkle shredded cheddar cheese over each serving. Serves 4 to 6.

Ham-Vegetable Chowder

A great recipe for leftover ham.

1 medium potato
1 cup (140 g) diced ham
2 280-g (10-ounce) cans
   cream of celery soup
½ litre carton chicken stock
3 cups (420 g) finely diced
   ham
1 425-g (15-ounce) can
   corn kernels
2 carrots, peeled, sliced
1 onion, coarsely chopped
1 teaspoon dried basil
1 teaspoon seasoned salt
280 g (10 ounces) frozen
   broccoli florets

- Cut potato into 2.5-cm (1-inch) pieces.

- Combine 1 teaspoon pepper and all ingredients except broccoli in large slow cooker.

- Cover and cook on low for 5 to 6 hours. Add broccoli to cooker and cook for an additional 1 hour. Serves 4 to 6.

TIP: If you don't like black specks in your chowder, use white pepper instead of black pepper.

Crab Chowder

2 small zucchini, thinly sliced
1 red capsicum, julienned
2 sticks celery, diagonally
    sliced
1 medium potato, cubed
2 tablespoons (30 g) butter,
    melted
1½ cups (375 ml) chicken stock
1 teaspoon seasoned salt
2 tablespoons (15 g) cornflour
3 cups (750 ml) milk
2 170-g (6-ounce) cans crabmeat,
    drained
85 g (3 ounces) cream cheese,
    cubed

- Place zucchini, capsicum, celery, potato, butter, stock and seasoned salt in sprayed slow cooker.

- Stir cornflour into milk in bowl; pour into slow cooker.

- Cover and cook on low for 3 to 4 hours.

- Turn heat to high, add crabmeat and cream cheese and stir until cream cheese melts. Serves 4.

Country Chicken Chowder

680 g (1½ pounds) boneless, skinless chicken breast halves
2 tablespoons (30 g) butter
2 280-g (10-ounce) cans creamy leek and potato soup
½ litre carton chicken stock
230 g (8 ounces) frozen corn kernels
1 onion, sliced
2 sticks celery, sliced
280 g (10 ounces) frozen peas and carrots, thawed
½ teaspoon dried thyme leaves
½ cup (125 ml) unthickened cream

- Cut chicken into 2.5-cm (1-inch) strips.

- Brown chicken strips in butter in frypan and transfer to large slow cooker.

- Add soup, stock, corn, onion, celery, peas and carrots, and thyme and stir.

- Cover and cook on low for 3 to 4 hours or until vegetables are tender.

- Turn off heat, stir in cream and set aside for about 10 minutes before serving. Serves 4 to 6.

Chicken Chowder

3 cups (420 g) cooked, cubed
  chicken
½ litre carton chicken stock
2 280-g (10-ounce) cans creamy
  leek and potato soup
1 large onion, chopped
3 sticks celery, sliced
  diagonally
455 g (16 ounces) frozen corn
  kernels, thawed
⅔ cup (150 ml) pouring
  cream

- Combine chicken, chicken stock, leek and potato soup, onion, celery, corn and ¾ cup (175 ml) water in 5 to 6-L (5 to 6-quart) slow cooker.

- Cover and cook on low for 3 to 4 hours.

- Add cream to slow cooker and heat for additional 15 minutes or until thoroughly hot. Serves 4 to 6.

Oyster Chowder

1 small red capsicum,
    seeded, chopped
1 onion, chopped
½ litre carton chicken stock
1 medium potato, cubed
1 fresh red chilli,
    seeded, finely chopped
230 g (8 ounces) shucked oysters
    with liquid
280 g (10 ounces)
    frozen corn kernels, thawed
1 teaspoon dried oregano
½ cup (125 ml) pouring cream

• Combine all ingredients except
  cream in slow cooker.

• Cover and cook on low for
  3 to 4 hours.

• When ready to serve, stir in
  cream. Serves 4.

Split-Pea and Ham Chowder

1 medium potato
3 cups (420 g) cooked, cubed
    ham
455 g (16 ounces) split
    peas, rinsed
1 310-g (11-ounce) can corn
    kernels
½ litre carton chicken stock
2 carrots, sliced
2 sticks celery, diagonally
    sliced
1 tablespoon (15 ml) dried onion
    flakes
1 teaspoon dried marjoram
    leaves
1 teaspoon seasoned salt

• Cut potato into small cubes and
  add to sprayed slow cooker.

• Add remaining ingredients plus
  3 cups (750 ml) water and
  1 teaspoon salt.

• Cover and cook on low for
  6 to 8 hours. Serves 4 to 6.

Corn-Ham Chowder

½ litre carton chicken stock
1 cup (250 ml) milk
1 280-g (10-ounce) can cream
  of celery soup
1 425-g (15-ounce) can
  creamed corn
1 425-g (15-ounce) can
  corn kernels
½ cup (30 g) instant mashed
  potato flakes
1 onion, chopped
2–3 cups 280–420 g cooked,
  chopped ham

- Combine stock, milk, soup, creamed corn, corn, potato flakes, onion and ham in 6-L (6-quart) slow cooker.

- Cover and cook on low for 4 to 5 hours.

- When ready to serve, season with a little salt and pepper. Serves 4 to 6.

Prawn and Ham Jambalaya

3 sticks celery, diagonally sliced
1 onion, chopped
1 red capsicum, seeded,
    chopped
1 green capsicum, seeded,
    chopped
2 425-g (15-ounce) cans
    stewed tomatoes
2 cups (280 g) cooked, cubed
    smoked ham
½ teaspoon cayenne pepper
1 tablespoon (15 ml) dried
    parsley flakes
2 teaspoons minced garlic
455 g (1 pound) peeled,
    veined prawns
Rice, cooked

- Combine celery, onion, capsicums, tomatoes, ham, cayenne pepper, parsley flakes, garlic and a little salt and pepper in sprayed slow cooker.

- Cover and cook on low for 7 to 8 hours or on high for 3 to 4 hours.

- Stir in prawns and cook on low for 1 hour.

- Serve over rice. Serves 4 to 6.

Prawn and Sausage Jambalaya

455 g (1 pound) cooked, smoked
    sausages
1 onion, chopped
1 green capsicum, chopped
2 teaspoons minced garlic
1 795-g (28-ounce) can diced
    tomatoes
1 tablespoon (15 ml)parsley
    flakes
½ teaspoon dried thyme leaves
1 teaspoon Cajun seasoning
¼ teaspoon cayenne pepper
455 g (1 pound) peeled, veined
    prawns
Rice, cooked

- Combine all ingredients except prawns and rice in sprayed slow cooker.

- Cover and cook on low for 6 to 8 hours or on high for 3 to 4 hours.

- Stir in prawns and cook on low for an additional 1 hour. Serve over rice. Serves 4 to 6.

Prawn and Chicken Jambalaya

4 chicken breast halves,
 cubed
1 795-g (28-ounce) can diced
 tomatoes
1 onion, chopped
1 green capsicum, seeded,
 chopped
½ litre carton chicken stock
½ cup (125 ml) dry white wine
 or cooking wine
2 teaspoons dried oregano
2 teaspoons Cajun seasoning
½ teaspoon cayenne pepper
455 g (1 pound) cooked, peeled,
 veined prawns
2 cups (370 g) cooked white rice

- Place all ingredients except prawns and rice in slow cooker and stir.

- Cover and cook on low for 6 to 8 hours.

- Turn heat to high, stir in prawns and rice and cook for an additional 15 to 20 minutes. Serves 4 to 6.

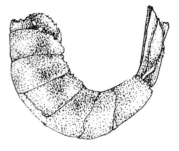

Veggies &
Side Dishes

Baked, Braised,
Crunched & Stewed

Veggies & Side Dishes Contents

Broccoli-Cheese Bake

¼ cup (55 g) butter, melted
1 280-g (10-ounce) can cream
   of mushroom soup
1 packet French onion soup
1 cup (95 g) instant rice
230 g (8 ounces) cubed cheddar
   cheese
560 g (20 ounces) frozen chopped
   broccoli florets, thawed

- Combine all ingredients, plus
  1 cup (250 ml) water in sprayed
  slow cooker and stir well.

- Cover and cook on high for
  2 to 3 hours. Serves 4 to 6.

Savoury Broccoli and Cauliflower

455 g (16 ounces) frozen broccoli
   florets, thawed
455 g (16 ounces) frozen
   cauliflower florets, thawed
2 280-g (10-ounce) cans
   cream of celery soup
6 slices bacon, cooked, crumbled

- Place broccoli and cauliflower
  in sprayed slow cooker. Sprinkle
  with a little salt and pepper.

- Spoon soup over top and
  sprinkle with bacon. Cover and
  cook on low for 3 to 4 hours.
  Serves 6 to 8.

Broccoli and Cheese

850 g (32 ounces) frozen broccoli
   florets, thawed
2 425-g (15-ounce) cans whole
   new potatoes, drained
2 280-g (10-ounce) cans
   cream of celery soup
½ cup (125 ml) milk
230 g (8 ounces) shredded
   cheddar cheese
1½ cups (90 g) cracker crumbs

- Place broccoli on plate, cut off stems and discard. Combine broccoli and potatoes in slow cooker.

- Combine soup and milk in saucepan, heat just enough to mix well and pour over broccoli and potatoes.

- Sprinkle half cheese and crumbs over broccoli.

- Cover and cook on low for 3 to 4 hours.

- When ready to serve, sprinkle remaining cheese and crumbs over top. Serves 6 to 8.

Company Broccoli

680 g (1½ pounds) fresh broccoli
  florets, trimmed well
1 280-g (10-ounce) can cream
  of chicken soup
½ cup (110 g) mayonnaise
1 230-g (8-ounce) shredded
  cheddar cheese
¼ cup (40 g) toasted slivered
  almonds

- Place broccoli in sprayed
  slow cooker.

- Combine chicken soup,
  mayonnaise, half cheese and
  ¼ cup (60 ml) water in bowl.
  Spoon over broccoli.

- Cover and cook on low for
  2 to 3 hours. When ready to
  serve, sprinkle remaining cheese
  over broccoli and top with
  toasted almonds. Serves 6 to 8.

Sunshine Green Beans

910 g (32 ounces) frozen whole
  green beans, thawed
2 280-g (10-ounce) cans
  cream of celery soup
1 onion, chopped
1 red capsicum, chopped
1 green capsicum, chopped
½ 115 g (4 ounces) can sliced
  water chestnuts
1 teaspoon seasoned salt

- Combine all ingredients plus
  ¼ cup (60 ml) water in large
  slow cooker and stir to mix well.

- Cover and cook on low for
  4 to 5 hours. Serves 6 to 8.

Southern Green Beans and Potatoes

6–8 medium new potatoes
with peels, sliced
5 cups (355 g) fresh whole green
beans, trimmed
2 tablespoons (30 ml) minced
onions
¼ cup (60 g) butter, melted
2 280-g (10-ounce) cans cream
of celery soup

- Place potatoes, green beans and minced onions in sprayed slow cooker.

- Pour melted butter over vegetables.

- Combine soups and ⅓ cup (75 ml) water in saucepan. Heat just enough to be able to mix soups and pour over vegetables.

- Cover and cook on low for 7 to 8 hours. Serves 6 to 8.

Green Beans to Enjoy

910 g (2 pounds) fresh green beans
1 onion, finely chopped
4 thick slices bacon
5–6 medium new (red) potatoes
1 teaspoon sugar

- Snap and wash green beans, place beans and onion in sprayed 5 to 6-L (5 to 6-quart) slow cooker.

- Cut bacon in 2.5-cm (1-inch) pieces and fry in frypan until crisp.

- Remove some of deeper 'eyes' in new potatoes and cut into quarters.

- Add cooked bacon pieces, potatoes and 1 cup (250 ml) water to slow cooker.

- Add about 1 teaspoon each of salt and sugar. (A touch of sugar always helps fresh vegetables.)

- Cover and cook on low for 3 to 4 hours. Serves 6 to 8.

Green Bean Revenge

2 425-g (16-ounce) frozen whole
  green beans, thawed
2 230-g (8-ounce) cans sliced
  water chestnuts, drained
455 g (16 ounces) cubed
  cheddar cheese
1 280-g (10-ounce) can tomatoes
2 green chillies, chopped
¼ cup (55 g) butter, melted
1 tablespoon (15 ml) chicken
  seasoning
1½ cups (85 g) slightly crushed
  potato chips

- Combine green beans, water chestnuts, cheese, tomatoes, green chillies, melted butter and seasoning in slow cooker and mix well.

- Cover and cook on low for 3 to 5 hours. Just before serving, cover top with crushed potato chips. Serves 6 to 8.

TIP: *If you would like this to be a one-dish meal, add 2 to 3 cups (280 to 420 g) cooked, cubed ham.*

Crunchy Green Beans

910 g (32 ounces) frozen whole
  green beans, thawed
3 sticks celery, diagonally sliced
1 red capsicum, julienned
2 310-g (11-ounce) cans sliced
  water chestnuts, drained
1 280-g (10-ounce) can cream of
  chicken soup
½ cup (85 g) slivered almonds
½ cup fried onion rings

- Combine green beans, celery,
  capsicum, water chestnuts,
  chicken soup and almonds in
  sprayed slow cooker.

- Cover and cook on low for
  2 to 4 hours. About 10 minutes
  before serving, top with fried
  onion rings. Serves 6 to 8.

Cajun Beans and Rice

455 g (1 pound) dry black or
  kidney beans
2 onions, chopped
2 teaspoons minced garlic
1 tablespoon (15 ml) ground
  cumin
½ litre carton chicken stock
1 cup (95 g) instant brown
  rice

- Place beans in saucepan, cover
  with water and soak overnight.

- Combine beans, onion, garlic,
  cumin, chicken stock,
  2 teaspoons salt and
  2 cups (500 ml) water to
  4 to 5-L (4 to 5-quart)
  slow cooker.

- Cover and cook on low for
  4 to 6 hours. Serves 6 to 8.

A Different Bean

3 425-g (15-ounce) cans kidney
   beans, rinsed, drained
3 425-g (15-ounce) cans
   cannellini beans, rinsed,
   drained
1 455-g (16-ounce) jar hot,
   thick-and-chunky salsa
½ cup (110 g) brown sugar

- Combine kidney beans,
  cannellini beans, salsa and
  brown sugar in 5 to 6-L (5 to
  6-quart) slow cooker.

- Cover and cook on low for
  3 to 4 hours. Serves 6 to 8.

TIP: *To include borlotti beans in
   this dish, use only 2 cans
   kidney beans and 1 can
   borlotti beans.*

Beans and More Beans

4 thick slices bacon, cooked
   crisp, crumbled
1 425-g (15-ounce) can kidney
   beans, drained
1 425-g (15-ounce) can butter
   beans with liquid
1 425-g (15-ounce) can borlotti
   beans with liquid
1 425-g (15-ounce) can cannellini
   beans with liquid
1 425-g (15-ounce) can baked
   beans with ham sauce
1 onion, chopped
¾ cup (205 g) chilli sauce
1 cup (220 g) brown sugar
1 tablespoon (15 ml)
   Worcestershire sauce

- Combine all ingredients in
  sprayed slow cooker and
  mix well.

- Cover and cook on low for
  5 to 6 hours. Serves 6 to 8.

Better Butter Beans

2 cups (200 g) sliced celery
2 onions, chopped
1 green capsicum, julienned
1 425-g (15-ounce) can
    stewed tomatoes
¼ cup (60 g) butter, melted
1 tablespoon (15 ml) chicken
    seasoning
3 425-g (15-ounce) cans butter
    beans, drained

- Combine all ingredients in slow cooker and mix well.

- Cover and cook on low for 3 to 4 hours. Serves 6 to 8.

TIP: You can make this a one-dish dinner; add 2 to 3 cups (280 to 420 g) cooked, cubed ham.

Italian Beans

2 425-g (15-ounce) cans
    chickpeas, drained
1 425-g (15-ounce) can red
    kidney beans, drained
1 425-g (15-ounce) can
    cannellini beans, drained
2 425-g (15-ounce) cans
    borlotti beans, drained
1 teaspoon Italian seasoning
30 g (1 ounce) French onion
    soup mix
1 teaspoon minced garlic
½ cup (125 ml) beef stock

- Combine all ingredients in slow cooker and stir well.

- Cover and cook on low for 5 to 6 hours or on high for 2 hours 30 minutes to 3 hours. Serves 6 to 8.

Creamy Limas

850 g (15 ounces) lima beans
1 280-g (10-ounce) can
   cream of celery
1 280-g (10-ounce) can cream of
   mushroom soup
1 red capsicum, cored, seeded,
   julienned
1 115-g (4-ounce) jar sliced
   mushrooms, drained
¼ cup (60 ml) milk
1 cup (115 g) shredded
   cheddar cheese

- Combine lima beans, soups, capsicum, mushrooms and ½ teaspoon salt in saucepan and heat just enough to mix well.

- Pour into sprayed 4 to 5-L (4 to 5-quart) slow cooker. Stir well.

- Cover and cook on low for 8 to 9 hours.

- Just before serving, stir in milk. Spoon limas to serving bowl and sprinkle cheese over top. Serves 6 to 8.

Chilli Frijoles

2 cups (525 g) dry borlotti beans
2 onions, finely chopped
2 tablespoons (30 ml) chilli
powder
1 teaspoon minced garlic
1 425-g (15-ounce) can tomato
soup
1½ pounds (680 g) lean minced
beef

• Soak beans overnight in water.
Drain and transfer beans to large
slow cooker. Add onion, chilli
powder, garlic, tomato soup and
8 cups (1.9 L) water.

• Brown beef in frypan, drain and
transfer to cooker.

• Cover and cook on low for 8 to
9 hours or until beans are tender
and stir occasionally. Stir in 1
teaspoon salt just before serving.
Serves 6 to 8.

TIP: If you forget to soak beans
overnight, here's Plan B.
Place beans in large saucepan
and cover with water. Bring
to the boil, turn off heat and
let stand for 1 hour.

Cinnamon Carrots

910 g (32 ounces) baby carrots
¾ cup (165 g) brown sugar
¼ cup (85 g) honey
½ cup (125 ml) orange juice
2 tablespoons (30 g) butter,
  melted
¾ teaspoon ground cinnamon

- Place carrots in sprayed 3 to 4-L (3 to 4-quart) slow cooker.

- Combine brown sugar, honey, orange juice, butter and cinnamon in bowl and mix well. Pour over carrots and mix so sugar-cinnamon mixture coats carrots.

- Cover and cook on low for 3 hours 30 minutes to 4 hours and stir twice during cooking time.

- About 20 minutes before serving, transfer carrots with slotted spoon to serving dish and cover to keep warm.

- Pour liquid from cooker into saucepan; boil for several minutes until liquid reduces by half. Spoon over carrots in serving dish. Serves 6 to 8.

Krazy Karrots

455 g (16 ounces) baby carrots
¼ cup (60 g) butter, melted
⅔ cup (150 g) brown sugar
1 30-g (1-ounce) packet French
onion soup mix

- Combine carrots, melted butter, brown sugar, soup mix and ¼ cup (60 ml) water in 4-L (4-quart) slow cooker and stir well.

- Cover and cook on low for 3 to 4 hours and stir occasionally. Serves 4.

Squash Combo

680 g (1½ pounds) small yellow
squash
680 g (1½ pounds) zucchini
1 teaspoon seasoned salt
¼ cup (60 g) butter, melted
½ cup (60 g) seasoned
breadcrumbs
½ cup (60 g) shredded cheddar
cheese

- Cut both squash and zucchini in small pieces.

- Place in sprayed slow cooker and sprinkle with seasoned salt and pepper.

- Pour melted butter over squash and sprinkle with breadcrumbs and cheese.

- Cover and cook on low for 5 to 6 hours. Serves 6 to 8.

Sunny Yellow Squash

910 g (2 pounds) medium yellow
   squash, sliced
2 onions, coarsely chopped
3 sticks celery, diagonally sliced
1 green capsicum, cored,
   seeded, julienned
230 g (8 ounces) cream cheese,
   cubed
1 teaspoon sugar
¼ cup (60 g) butter, melted
1 280-g (10-ounce) can cream
   of celery soup
1½ cups (180 g) crushed
   croutons

- Combine all ingredients, except breadcrumbs, in slow cooker and mix well. Add 1 teaspoon each of salt and pepper.

- Cover and cook on low for 3 to 4 hours. Before serving, sprinkle top with breadcrumbs. Serves 6 to 8.

TIP: If you don't like black specks, use white pepper instead of black pepper.

Golden Squash

**455 g (1 pound) yellow squash,
thinly sliced**
**455 g (1 pound) zucchini,
thinly sliced**
3 sticks celery, sliced
1 onion, chopped
**1 280-g (10-ounce) can cream
of chicken soup**
230 g (8 ounces) sour cream
3 tablespoons (20 g) flour
**170 g (6 ounces) seasoned stuffing
mix**
½ cup (115 g) butter, melted

- Combine squash, zucchini, celery, onion and soup in large bowl.

- In separate bowl, mix sour cream with flour and stir into vegetables.

- Toss stuffing with melted butter in bowl and spoon half into slow cooker.

- Top with vegetables and spoon remaining stuffing on top.

- Cover and cook on low for 5 to 7 hours. Serves 6 to 8.

Super Corn

2 425-g (15-ounce) cans
   corn kernels
2 425-g (15-ounce) cans
   creamed corn
½ cup (115 g) butter,
   melted
230 g (8 ounces) sour cream
230 g (8 ounces) bread mix

- Combine all ingredients in large
  bowl and mix well.

- Pour into sprayed slow cooker,
  cover and cook on low for
  4 to 5 hours. Serves 6 to 8.

TIP: Make this a one-dish meal
   by adding 2 to 3 cups
   (280 to 420 g) leftover,
   cubed ham.

Yummy Corn

230 g (8 ounces) and
   85 g (3 ounces)
   cream cheese
½ cup (115 g) butter, melted
910-g (32 ounces) frozen corn
   kernels, thawed

- Turn sprayed 4-L (4-quart) slow
  cooker to high and add cream
  cheese and butter.

- Cook just until cheese and butter
  melt and stir. Add corn and a
  little salt and pepper.

- Cover and cook on low for 1
  hour 30 minutes to 2 hours.
  Serves 4 to 6.

Creamed Peas and Potatoes

910 g (2 pounds) small (red)
   new potatoes with
   peels, quartered
455 g (16 ounces) frozen green
   peas, thawed
2 280-g (10-ounce) cans
   cream of chicken soup
½ cup (125 ml) milk

- Sprinkle potatoes with a little salt and pepper, place in sprayed slow cooker and place peas on top.

- Combine soup and milk in saucepan, heat just enough to mix well and spoon over peas.

- Cover and cook on low for 4 to 5 hours. Serves 6 to 8.

Creamed Cheese Spinach

560 g (20 ounces) frozen
   chopped spinach
910 g (32 ounces) cottage
   cheese
1½ cups (170 g) shredded
   cheddar cheese
3 eggs, beaten
¼ cup (60 g) butter, melted
¼ cup (30 g) flour

- Squeeze spinach between paper towels to completely remove excess moisture.

- Combine all ingredients in bowl and mix well. Spoon into sprayed slow cooker.

- Cover and cook on high for 1 hour, change heat to low and cook for an additional 3 to 5 hours or until knife inserted in centre comes out clean. Serves 4 to 6.

Cheese-Please Spinach

**735 g (26 ounces) chopped
   spinach, thawed, drained**
**230 g (8 ounces) cream cheese,
   cubed, softened**
**280-g (10-ounce) can
   cream of chicken soup**
1 egg, beaten
**230 g (8 ounces) shredded
   cheddar cheese**

- Squeeze spinach between paper towels to completely remove excess moisture.

- Combine spinach, cream cheese, chicken soup, egg and a little salt and pepper in large bowl. Spoon into sprayed slow cooker.

- Cover and cook on low for 3 to 4 hours.

- Before serving, stir in cheddar cheese. Serves 4 to 6.

Healthy Veggies

455 g (16 ounces) frozen broccoli,
    cauliflower florets and carrots
2 medium zucchini, halved
    lengthwise, sliced
30 g (1 ounce) French onion
    soup mix
2 tablespoons (30 g) butter,
    melted

- Place broccoli, cauliflower and
  carrots, and zucchini in 4-L
  (4-quart) slow cooker.

- Combine soup mix, melted
  butter and ½ cup (125 ml) water
  in bowl, spoon over vegetables
  and stir.

- Cover and cook on low for
  2 to 3 hours. Serves 4.

Harvest-Vegetable Casserole

3–4 medium new (red) potatoes
    with peels, sliced
2 onions, sliced
3 carrots, sliced
2 cups (140 g) chopped green
    cabbage
¼ cup (60 ml) Italian dressing
455 g (1 pound) chorizo sausage
425-g (15-ounce) can Italian
    stewed tomatoes

- Place potatoes, onions, carrots,
  cabbage and Italian dressing in
  large, sprayed slow cooker.

- Cut sausage into 2.5-cm
  (1-inch) pieces and place on top
  of vegetables.

- Drizzle stewed tomatoes in even
  layers over vegetables.

- Cover and cook on low for
  6 to 8 hours or until vegetables
  are tender. Serves 4 to 6.

Golden Veggies

455 g (16 ounces) frozen
    cauliflower florets, thawed
1 425-g (15-ounce) can corn
    kernels
340 g (¾ pound) small yellow
    squash, chopped
¼ cup (60 g) butter, melted
2 280-g (10-ounce) cans
    cream of celery soup
6 slices bacon, cooked, crumbled

- Place cauliflower, corn and squash in sprayed slow cooker and sprinkle with a little salt and pepper.

- Pour melted butter over vegetables and spoon soup on top. Sprinkle with crumbled bacon.

- Cover and cook on low for 4 to 5 hours. Serves 4 to 6.

Four Veggie Bake

280 g (10 ounces) frozen broccoli
    florets, thawed
280 g (10 ounces) frozen
    cauliflower, thawed
280 g (10 ounces) frozen brussels
    sprouts
4 small yellow squash, sliced
1 280-g (10-ounce) can cream of
    mushroom soup
455 g (16 ounces) cubed cheddar
    cheese

- Place vegetables in sprayed slow cooker.

- Layer soup and cheese on top of vegetables.

- Cover and cook on low for 3 to 4 hours. Serves 4 to 6.

California Vegetables

455 g (16 ounces) frozen
  vegetable mix, thawed
280 g (10 ounces) frozen green
  peas, thawed
280 g (10 ounces) frozen corn
  kernels, thawed
2 280-g (10-ounce) cans cream
  of mushroom soup
1 cup (95 g) instant white rice
230 g (8 ounces) cubed
  cheddar cheese
1 cup (250 ml) milk
2 tablespoons (30 g) butter,
  melted
1 teaspoon seasoned salt

- Place all vegetables in large, sprayed slow cooker.

- Combine soup, rice, cheese, milk, butter, seasoned salt and 1 cup (250 ml) water in saucepan, heat just enough to mix and pour over vegetables.

- Cover and cook on low for 4 to 5 hours. Stir before serving. Serves 6 to 8.

Creamed New Potatoes

910 g (2–2½ pounds) new (red) potatoes with peels, quartered
230 g (8 ounces) cream cheese, softened
1 280-g (10-ounce) can cream of celery soup
30 g (1 ounce) French onion soup mix
1 cup (250 ml) milk

- Place potatoes in 6-L (6-quart) slow cooker.

- Beat cream cheese until creamy and fold in celery soup, soup mix and milk. Stir into potatoes.

- Cover and cook on low for 3 to 4 hours or until potatoes are well done. Serves 4 to 6.

Pretty Parsley Potatoes

910 g (2 pounds) new (red) potatoes with peels, quartered
¼ cup (60 ml) canola oil
10 g (0.4 ounce) French onion soup mix
¼ cup (15 g) chopped fresh parsley

- Place potatoes, oil, soup mix and ¼ cup (60 ml) water in 4 to 5-L (4 to 5-quart) slow cooker and toss to coat potatoes.

- Cover and cook on low for 3 to 4 hours or until potatoes are tender.

- When ready to serve, sprinkle parsley over potatoes and toss. Serves 4 to 6.

Potatoes al Grande

6 medium potatoes,
peeled
230 g (8 ounces) shredded
cheddar cheese
280-g (10-ounce) can cream
of chicken soup
¼ cup (60 g) butter, melted
230 g (8 ounces) sour cream
1 cup (85 g) fried onion rings

- Cut potatoes in 2.5-cm (1-inch) strips. Toss potatoes with a little salt and pepper plus 1½ cups (230 g) cheese. Place in slow cooker.

- Combine soup, melted butter and 2 tablespoons (30 ml) water in saucepan and heat just enough to pour over potato mixture.

- Cover and cook on low for 6 to 8 hours or until potatoes are tender.

- Stir in sour cream and remaining cheese.

- When ready to serve, sprinkle onion rings over top of potatoes. Serves 4 to 6.

Roasted New Potatoes

**18–20 new (red) potatoes
with peels
¼ cup (60 g) butter, melted
1 tablespoon (15 ml) dried
parsley
½ teaspoon garlic powder
½ teaspoon paprika**

- Combine all ingredients plus
½ teaspoon each of salt and
pepper in sprayed slow cooker
and mix well.

- Cover and cook on low for
7 hours or on high for
3 hours 30 minutes to 4 hours.

- When ready to serve, remove
potatoes with slotted spoon to
serving dish and cover to
keep warm.

- Add about 2 tablespoons (30 ml)
water to drippings and stir until
they blend well.

- Pour mixture over potatoes.
Serves 4 to 6.

Good Old Cheesy Potatoes

795 g (28 ounces) frozen hash browns, thawed
2 280-g (10-ounce) cans cream of chicken soup
230 g (8 ounces) sour cream
½ cup (115 g) butter, melted
230 g (8 ounces) shredded cheddar cheese
2 tablespoons (30 ml) dried parsley
2 cups (120 g) dry stuffing mix

- Combine hash browns, soup, sour cream, ¼ cup (57 g) melted butter, cheese, parsley and 1 teaspoon salt in large bowl and mix well.

- Spoon mixture into large slow cooker. Sprinkle stuffing mix over hash browns mixture and drizzle remaining butter over stuffing.

- Cover and cook on low for 7 to 9 hours or on high for 3 to 4 hours. Serves 4 to 6.

Glory Potatoes

1 280-g (10-ounce) can cream of
    chicken soup
230 g (8 ounces) sour cream
910 g (2 pounds) potatoes,
    peeled, cubed
230 g (8 ounces) shredded
    cheddar cheese
1 cup (55 g) crushed potato
    chips

- Combine soup, sour cream,
  ¼ cup (60 ml) water and a little
  salt and pepper in bowl.

- Combine potatoes and cheese
  in 5-L (5-quart) slow cooker.
  Spoon soup-sour cream mixture
  over potatoes.

- Cover and cook on low for
  8 to 9 hours.

- When ready to serve, sprinkle
  crushed potato chips over
  potatoes. Serves 4 to 6.

Easy Baked Potatoes

6 medium starchy potatoes
    with peels
¼–½ cup (60–125 ml) canola oil
Butter
Sour cream

- Pierce potatoes with fork.
  Brush potato skins with oil and
  sprinkle a little salt and pepper
  on potato skins.

- Wrap potatoes individually in
  foil and place in large
  slow cooker.

- Cover and cook on low for
  7 to 8 hours or until potatoes
  are tender.

- Prepare assorted toppings such
  as: shredded cheese, salsa, dip,
  chopped spring onions, bacon
  bits, chopped boiled eggs, etc.
  Serves 6.

Dressed-Up Hash Browns

**740 g (26 ounces) frozen
   hash browns**
Canola oil
**2–3 cups (280–420 g) chopped
   cooked ham**
455 g (16 ounces) sour cream
**230 g (8 ounces) shredded
   cheddar cheese**
1 cup (85 g) fried onion rings

- Cook hash browns in a little oil in large frypan. Transfer to 5 to 6-L (5 to 6-quart) slow cooker.

- Combine ham, sour cream and cheese in bowl and mix into hash browns.

- Cover and cook on low for 2 to 3 hours.

- Dress potatoes up by sprinkling onion rings on top of cheese. Serves 4 to 6.

Company Potatoes

6 medium potatoes,
   peeled, sliced
1 packet scalloped potato mix
55 g (4 ounces) shredded cheddar
   cheese
1 cup (250 ml) milk
6 tablespoons (85 g) butter,
   melted
230 g (½ pound) bacon, cooked
   crisp, crumbled

- Place potatoes, scalloped potato mix and cheese in sprayed slow cooker. Combine milk, butter and 4¼ cups (1.1 L) water in bowl and pour over potatoes.

- Cover and cook on low for 4 to 5 hours.

- When ready to serve, sprinkle crumbled bacon over top of potatoes. Serves 4 to 6.

Cheezy Potatoes

795 g (28 ounces) frozen
   diced potatoes with
   onions, thawed
230 g (8 ounces) shredded
   cheddar cheese
1 280-g (10-ounce) can cream
   of celery soup
230 g (8 ounces) sour cream

- Combine potatoes, cheese, soup, sour cream and 1 teaspoon pepper in sprayed 5 to 6-L (5 to 6-quart) slow cooker and mix well.

- Cover and cook on low 4 to 6 hours. Stir well before serving. Serves 6 to 8.

Sweet Potatoes and Pineapple

3 sweet potatoes, diced
½ 570-g (20-ounce) can
    pineapple pieces
2 tablespoons (30 g) butter,
    melted
½ cup (110 g) brown sugar
½ teaspoon ground
    cinnamon
1 cup (220 g) brown sugar
3 tablespoons (40 g) butter,
    melted
½ cup (60 g) flour
1 cup (110 g) coarsely chopped
    nuts

- Place sweet potatoes, pineapple pieces, melted butter, brown sugar and cinnamon in sprayed 4 to 5-L (4 to 5-quart) slow cooker and lightly stir.

- Cover and cook on low for 2 to 3 hours. Serves 6 to 8.

- While potatoes cook, combine topping ingredients in bowl, spread out on foil-lined baking pan and bake at 175° C (350° F) for 15 to 20 minutes.

- When ready to serve, sprinkle topping over sweet potatoes.

Cheesy Ranch Potatoes

910 g (2½ pounds) new (red)
  potatoes with peels,
  quartered
1 onion, cut into 8 wedges
1 280-g (10-ounce) can cream of
  celery soup
230 g (8 ounces) sour cream
30 g (1 ounce) French onion
  soup mix
Chopped fresh parsley, optional

- Place potatoes and onion in
  sprayed 4 to 5-L (4 to 5-quart)
  slow cooker.

- Combine celery soup, sour
  cream and soup mix in
  bowl and whisk well to
  mix. Spoon over
  potato-onion mixture.

- Cover and cook on low for
  6 to 7 hours.

- To serve, sprinkle chopped fresh
  parsley over potato mixture.
  Serves 4 to 6.

Glazed Sweet Potatoes

3 sweet potatoes, diced
¼ cup (60 g) butter, melted
2 cups (440 g) brown sugar
⅓ cup (75 ml) orange juice
½ teaspoon ground cinnamon

- Place sweet potatoes in 4 to 5-L
  (4 to 5-quart) slow cooker.

- Add butter, brown sugar, orange
  juice, a little salt and a sprinkle
  of cinnamon and stir well.

- Cover and cook on low for
  4 to 5 hours. Serves 4 to 6.

Hoppin' John

2 cups black-eyed peas
1 onion, chopped
170 g (6 ounces) instant tomato
    basil rice
2 cups (280 g) cooked,
    chopped ham
2 tablespoons (30 g) butter,
    melted

- In slow cooker, combine peas, onion, rice mix, ham, butter and 2½ cups (600 ml) water and mix well.

- Cover and cook on low for 2 to 4 hours. Serves 6 to 8.

Spicy Spanish Rice

1½ cups (280 g) white rice
1 280-g (10-ounce) can diced
    tomatoes
2 green chillies, chopped
1 425-g (15-ounce) can stewed
    tomatoes
30 g (1 ounce) taco seasoning
1 large onion, chopped

- Combine all ingredients plus 2 cups (500 ml) water in 5-L (5-quart) slow cooker and stir well.

- Cover and cook on low for 5 to 7 hours. (The flavour will go through the rice better if you stir 2 or 3 times during cooking time.) Serves 4.

TIP: Make this a main dish by slicing 1 pound (455 g) Polish sausage slices to rice mixture.

Delicious Risotto Rice

1½ cups (280 g) Italian
   risotto rice
1½ litres chicken stock
3 tablespoons (40 g) butter,
   melted
1½ cups (110 g) sliced, fresh
   mushrooms
1 cup (100 g) sliced celery

- Combine rice, stock, butter,
  mushrooms and celery in
  4 to 5-L (4 to 5-quart)
  slow cooker.

- Cover and cook on low for
  2 to 3 hours or until rice is
  tender. Serves 4 to 6.

Crunchy Couscous

When rice is boring, try couscous.

280 g (10 ounces) couscous
2 cups (200 g) sliced celery
1 red capsicum, seeded, chopped
1 yellow capsicum,
   seeded, chopped
1 455-g (16-ounce) jar creamy
   alfredo sauce

- Combine couscous, celery,
  capsicums, alfredo sauce and
  1½ cups (375 ml) water in
  5-L (5-quart) slow cooker and
  mix well.

- Cover and cook on low for
  2 hours, stir once or twice.

- Check slow cooker to make
  sure celery and capsicums are
  cooked, but still crunchy.
  Serves 4 to 6.

Carnival Couscous

155 g (5.7 ounces) couscous
1 chicken stock cube
1 red capsicum, seeded, julienned
1 green capsicum,
    seeded, julienned
2 small yellow squash,
    sliced
455 g (16 ounces) frozen mixed
    vegetables, thawed
1 280-g (10-ounce) can French
    onion soup
¼ cup (60 g) butter, melted
½ teaspoon (2 ml) seasoned salt

- Combine all ingredients with
  1½ cups (375 ml) water in
  sprayed slow cooker and
  mix well.

- Cover and cook on low for
  2 to 4 hours. Serves 4.

St. Pat's Pasta

340 g (12 ounces) fettuccini
    (medium egg noodles)
1 cup (250 ml) unthickened
    cream
280 g (10 ounces) frozen chopped
    spinach, thawed
6 tablespoons (85 g) butter,
    melted
2 teaspoons seasoned salt
1½ cups (170 g) shredded
    cheddar cheese

- Cook pasta according to package
  directions and drain.

- Place in 5 to 6-L (5 to 6-quart)
  slow cooker. Add cream,
  spinach, butter and seasoned
  salt and stir until they
  blend well.

- Cover and cook on low for
  2 to 3 hours.

- When ready to serve, fold in
  cheese. Serves 4.

Cheese-Spaghetti and Spinach

200 g (7 ounces) spaghetti, broken
2 tablespoons (30 g) butter
230 g (8 ounces) sour cream
1 cup (115 g) shredded cheddar cheese
230 g (8 ounces) Colby cheese
340 g (12 ounces) frozen, chopped spinach, thawed, well drained
1 cup (170 g) fried onions

- Cook pasta according to package directions, drain and stir in butter until it melts.

- Combine sour cream, cheddar cheese, half Colby cheese, spinach and half cup onions in large bowl.

- Fold into pasta and spoon into sprayed slow cooker.

- Cover and cook on low for 2 to 4 hours.

- When ready to serve, sprinkle remaining Colby cheese and fried onion rings over top. Serves 4.

TIP: Squeeze spinach between paper towels to completely remove excess moisture.

Beef

Roasted, Smothered & Chopped

Beef Contents

Savoury Steak

Great sauce with mashed potatoes.

**680 g (1½ pounds) lean round
steak**
1 onion, halved, sliced
**2 280-g (10-ounce) cans
mushroom soup**
**1½ cups (360 ml) hot,
thick-and-chunky salsa**

- Trim fat from steak and cut into serving-size pieces.

- Sprinkle with 1 teaspoon (5 ml) pepper and place in sprayed 5 to 6-L (5 to 6-quart) slow cooker.

- Place onion slices over steak.

- Combine mushroom soup and salsa in bowl and mix well. Spoon over steak and onions.

- Cover and cook on low for 7 to 8 hours. Serves 4 to 6.

Swiss Steak

**455–680 g (1–1½ pounds)
boneless, round steak**
½ teaspoon seasoned salt
½ teaspoon seasoned pepper
**8–10 medium new (red)
potatoes with peels, halved**
1 cup (135 g) baby carrots
1 onion, sliced
**1 425-g (15-ounce) can
stewed tomatoes**
**1 340-g (12-ounce) carton
beef gravy**

- Cut steak in 6 to 8 serving-size pieces, season with seasoned salt and pepper and brown in non-stick frypan.

- Layer steak pieces, potatoes, carrots and onion in slow cooker.

- Combine tomatoes and beef gravy in bowl and spoon over vegetables.

- Cover and cook on low for 7 to 8 hours. Serves 4 to 6.

Pepper Steak

680 g (1½ pounds) round steak
Canola oil
¼ cup (60 ml) soy sauce
1 onion, sliced
1 teaspoon minced garlic
1 teaspoon sugar
¼ teaspoon ground ginger
1 425-g (15-ounce) can stewed
   tomatoes
2 green capsicums, cored,
   seeded, julienned
1 stock cube beef
1 tablespoon (15 ml) cornflour
Rice or noodles, cooked

- Slice beef in strips, brown in frypan with a little oil and place in oval slow cooker.

- Combine soy sauce, onion, garlic, sugar and ginger in bowl and pour over beef.

- Cover and cook on low for 5 to 6 hours.

- Stir in tomatoes, capsicums and stock cube and cook for an additional 1 hour.

- Combine cornflour and ¼ cup water (60 ml) in cup and stir into cooker.

- Continue cooking until liquid thickens.

- Serve over rice or noodles. Serves 4 to 6.

Spicy Swiss Steak

**680 g (1½ pounds) boneless,
  beef round steak**
**115 g (4 ounces) spicy
  bratwurst**
2 small onions
**2 tablespoons (35 g)
  quick-cooking
  tapioca (or sago)**
1 teaspoon dried thyme
**2 425-g (15-ounce) cans
  stewed tomatoes**
2 teaspoons paprika
Noodles, cooked

- Trim fat from steak and cut into 4 serving-size pieces.

- Brown steak and bratwurst in frypan. Drain and place in sprayed 4 to 5-L (4 to 5-quart) slow cooker.

- Slice onions and separate into rings.

- Cover meat with onions and sprinkle with tapioca, thyme, a little salt and pepper. Pour stewed tomatoes over onion and seasonings.

- Cover and cook on low for 5 to 8 hours.

- Serve over noodles. Serves 4 to 6.

Stroganoff

910 g (2 pounds) beef round
**   steak**
¾ cup (90 g) flour
½ teaspoon mustard
2 onions, thinly sliced
230 g (½ pound) fresh
**   mushrooms, sliced**
1½ cups (375 ml) beef stock
¼ cup (60 ml) dry white wine or
**   cooking wine**
230 g (8 ounces) sour cream

- Trim excess fat from steak and cut into 8-cm (3-inch) strips about 1.2 cm (½ inch) wide.

- Combine ½ cup (60 ml) flour, mustard and a little salt and pepper in bowl and toss with steak strips.

- Place strips in sprayed, oval slow cooker.

- Cover with onions and mushrooms. Add beef stock and wine. Cover and cook on low for 8 to 10 hours.

- Just before serving, combine sour cream and ¼ cup (60 ml) flour in bowl.

- Stir into cooker and cook for an additional 10 to 15 minutes or until stroganoff thickens slightly. Serves 4 to 6.

Teriyaki Steak

680–910 g (1½–2 pounds) flank steak
1 425-g (15-ounce) can sliced pineapple with juice
1 tablespoon (15 ml) Worcestershire sauce
⅓ cup (75 g) brown sugar
3 tablespoons (45 ml) soy sauce
½ teaspoon ground ginger
½ litre (14 ounces) carton chicken stock
1 cup (200 g) long grain converted rice

- Roll flank steak, tie in place and cut into 7 to 8 individual steaks.

- Combine ½ cup (125 ml) pineapple juice, Worcestershire sauce, brown sugar, soy sauce and ginger in bowl large enough for marinade to cover individual steaks.

- Add steak rolls and marinate for 1 hour in sauce.

- Pour chicken stock into sprayed slow cooker.

- Add rice and ¾ cup (175 ml) water. Place steaks over rice and stock.

- Cover and cook on low for 8 to 10 hours. Serves 4 to 6.

Mushroom-Round Steak

680–910 g (1½–2 pounds) round
  steak
30 g (1 ounce) French onion
  soup mix
½ cup (125 ml) dry red wine
230 g (8 ounces) fresh
  mushrooms, sliced
1 280-g (10-ounce) can
  mushroom soup

- Cut round steak in serving-size
  pieces and place in sprayed, oval
  slow cooker.

- Combine soup mix, red wine,
  mushrooms, mushroom soup and
  ½ cup (125 ml) water in bowl,
  spoon over steak pieces.

- Cover and cook on low for
  7 to 8 hours. Serves 4 to 6.

O'Brian's Hash

3 cups (420 g) cooked, cubed
  beef roast
795 g (28 ounces) frozen hash
  browns, thawed
Canola oil
1 455-g (16-ounce) jar salsa
1 tablespoon (15 ml) seasoning
1 cup (116 g) shredded
  cheddar cheese

- Place beef in large, sprayed
  slow cooker.

- Brown hash browns in a little oil
  in large frypan. Stir in salsa and
  seasoning and transfer to slow
  cooker.

- Cover and cook on high for
  4 to 5 hours.

- When ready to serve, sprinkle
  cheese over top. Serves 4.

Italian Steak

455 g (1 pound) round steak,
cubed
2 cups (145 g) fresh mushroom
halves
1 425-g (15-ounce) can Italian
stewed tomatoes
1½ cups (355 ml) beef stock
½ cup (125 ml) red wine
2 teaspoons Italian seasoning
3 tablespoons (50 g)
quick-cooking
tapioca (or sago)
Linguine (thin egg noodles),
cooked

- Place beef in sprayed 4 to 5-L (4 to 5-quart) slow cooker.

- Combine mushrooms, tomatoes, beef stock, wine, Italian seasoning, tapioca and a little salt and pepper in bowl. Pour over steak.

- Cover and cook on low for 8 to 10 hours.

- Serve over linguine. Serves 4.

Cola Roast

1.8 kg (4 pounds) chuck roast
340 g (12 ounces) chilli sauce
1 onion, chopped
1 340-g (12-ounce) can cola
1 tablespoon (15 ml)
Worcestershire sauce

- Score roast in several places and fill each slit with a little salt and pepper.

- Sear roast in frypan on all sides. Place in 5-L (5-quart) slow cooker.

- Combine chilli sauce, onion, cola and Worcestershire sauce in bowl and mix well. Pour over roast.

- Cover and cook on low for 8 to 9 hours. Serves 6 to 8.

Beefy Onion Dinner

455–680 g (1–1½ pounds) round steak
1 onion
2 cups (145 g) fresh sliced mushrooms
1 280-g (10-ounce) can mushroom soup
170 g (6 ounces) herb stuffing mix
½ cup (115 g) butter, melted

- Cut beef into 5 to 6 serving-size pieces.

- Slice onion and separate into rings.

- Place steak pieces in oval slow cooker and top with onions and mushrooms.

- Pour soup over ingredients in cooker.

- Cover and cook on low for 7 to 9 hours.

- Just before serving, combine stuffing mix with seasoning packet, butter and ½ cup (125 ml) liquid from cooker and toss to mix.

- Place stuffing mixture on top of steak and increase heat to high.

- Cover and cook for an additional 15 minutes or until stuffing is fluffy. Serves 4 to 6.

Beef Roulades

**680 g (1½ pounds) beef flank
   steak**
5 slices bacon
**¾ cup (120 g) finely chopped
   onion**
**1 115-g (4-ounce) can
   mushroom pieces**
**1 tablespoon (15 ml)
   Worcestershire sauce**
⅓ cup (40 g) breadcrumbs
1 teaspoon Italian seasoning
340 g (12 ounces) beef gravy

- Cut steak into 4 to 6 serving-size pieces. Cut bacon into small pieces and combine with onion, mushrooms, Worcestershire sauce, seasoning and breadcrumbs in bowl.

- Place about ½ cup (125 ml) onion mixture on each piece of steak.

- Roll meat and secure ends with toothpicks. Dry beef rolls with paper towels. In frypan, brown steak rolls and transfer to sprayed slow cooker.

- Pour gravy evenly over steaks to thoroughly moisten. Cover and cook on low for 7 to 9 hours. Serves 4 to 6.

TIP: This meal is great served with mashed potatoes. You can also try instant mashed potatoes as a time saver.

Beef Tips over Noodles

½ cup (60 g) plus 3
    tablespoons flour
1.4 kg (3 pounds) beef tips
230 g (8 ounces) fresh
    mushrooms, sliced
1 bunch fresh spring
    onions, chopped
1 small red capsicum,
    seeded, chopped
¼ cup (70 g) tomato sauce
½ litre carton beef stock
1 tablespoon (15 ml)
    Worcestershire sauce
Noodles, cooked

- Coat beef tips with ½ cup (60 g) flour in bowl and transfer to sprayed slow cooker.

- Add mushrooms, onion, capsicum, tomato sauce, stock, Worcestershire sauce and a little salt and pepper.

- Cover and cook on low for 8 to 9 hours. About 1 hour before serving, turn heat to high.

- Combine remaining flour with ¼ cup (60 ml) water in small bowl, stir into cooker and cook until liquid thickens.

- Serve over noodles. Serves 6 to 8.

Beef Tips over Pasta

**910 g (2–2½ pounds) lean, beef
    stew meat
2 cups (320 g) small whole onions
1 green capsicum, seeded
1 170-g (6-ounce) jar pitted
    Greek olives or black olives
½ cup (30 g) sun-dried tomatoes
    in oil, drained, chopped
1 795-g (28-ounce) jar tomato
    pasta sauce
230 g (8 ounces) pasta twirls,
    cooked**

- Place beef and onions in sprayed 4 to 5-L (4 to 5-quart) slow cooker.

- Cut capsicum into 2.5-cm (1-inch) cubes and add to slow cooker.

- Add olives and tomatoes and pour pasta sauce over top.

- Cover and cook on low for 8 to 10 hours.

- Serve over pasta. Serves 4 to 6.

Pot Roast and Veggies

910 g (2 pounds) chuck roast
4–5 medium potatoes,
  peeled, quartered
4 large carrots, quartered
1 onion, quartered
½ litre carton beef stock
2 tablespoons (15 g) cornflour

- Trim fat from pieces of roast. Cut roast into 2 equal pieces.

- Brown pieces of roast in frypan. (Coat pieces with flour, salt and pepper if you'd like a little 'coating' on the outside.)

- Place potatoes, carrots and onion in sprayed 4 to 5-L (4 to 5-quart) slow cooker and mix well. Place browned beef over vegetables.

- Pour 1½ cups (375 ml) stock over beef and vegetables. Save remaining stock and refrigerate.

- Cover and cook on low for 8 to 9 hours. About 5 minutes before serving, remove beef and vegetables with slotted spoon and place on serving platter. Cover to keep warm.

- Pour liquid from slow cooker into medium saucepan.

- Blend remaining ½ cup (125 ml) stock and cornflour in bowl until smooth and add to liquid in saucepan. Boil for 1 minute and stir constantly.

- Serve gravy with roast and veggies and season with a little salt and pepper, if desired. Serves 4 to 6.

Sweet-and-Sour Beef

910 g (2 pounds) boneless chuck roast
½ cup (60 g) flour
Canola oil
1 onion, sliced
½ cup (135 g) chilli sauce
¾ cup (165 g) brown sugar
¼ cup (60 ml) red wine vinegar
1 tablespoon (15 ml) Worcestershire sauce
455 g (16 ounces) baby carrots

- Cut beef into 2.5-cm (1-inch) cubes and dredge in flour and a little salt and pepper.

- Brown beef in a little oil in frypan and place in sprayed slow cooker.

- Add remaining ingredients, except carrots, and 1 cup (250 ml) water.

- Cover and cook on low for 7 to 8 hours.

- Add carrots and cook for an additional 1 hour 30 minutes. Serves 4 to 6.

Old-Time Pot Roast

910 g (2–2½ pounds) boneless rump roast
5 medium potatoes, peeled, quartered
455 g (16 ounces) peeled baby carrots
2 medium onions, quartered
280-g (10-ounce) can mushroom soup
½ teaspoon dried basil
½ teaspoon seasoned salt

- Brown roast on all sides in large, non-stick frypan.

- Place potatoes, carrots and onions in sprayed 4 to 5-L (4 to 5-quart) slow cooker.

- Place browned roast on top of vegetables.

- Combine soup, basil and seasoned salt in bowl and pour mixture over meat and vegetables.

- Cover and cook on low for 9 to 11 hours. Serves 4 to 6.

TIP: To serve, transfer roast and vegetables to serving plate. Stir juices remaining in slow cooker and spoon over roast and vegetables.

Beef Tips and Mushrooms Supreme

2 280-g (10-ounce) cans
mushroom soup
½ litre carton beef stock
1 tablespoon (15 ml) steak
seasoning
2 115-g (4-ounce) cans sliced
mushrooms, drained
910 g (2 pounds) round
steak, cut in slices
Noodles
230 g (8 ounces) sour cream

- Combine soups, beef stock, steak seasoning and sliced mushrooms in bowl. Place in slow cooker and stir to blend.

- Add slices of beef and stir well.

- Cover and cook on low for 4 to 5 hours.

- When ready to serve, cook noodles, drain, add salt and a little butter.

- Stir sour cream into sauce in slow cooker. Spoon sauce and beef over noodles. Serves 4 to 6.

Herb-Crusted Beef Roast

910 g–1.4 kg (2–3 pounds) beef rump roast
¼ cup (15 g) chopped fresh parsley
¼ cup (15 g) chopped fresh oregano leaves
½ teaspoon dried rosemary leaves
1 teaspoon minced garlic
1 tablespoon (15 ml) canola oil
6 slices thick-cut bacon

- Rub roast with a little salt and pepper.

- Combine parsley, oregano, rosemary, garlic and oil in small bowl and press mixture on top and sides of roast.

- Place roast in slow cooker. Place bacon over top of beef and tuck ends under bottom.

- Cover and cook on low for 6 to 8 hours. Serves 4 to 6.

Classic Beef Roast

1.4–1.8 kg (3–4 pounds) beef chuck roast
30 g (1 ounce) French onion soup mix
2 280-g (10-ounce) cans cream of mushroom soup
3–4 medium potatoes, quartered

- Place roast in large, sprayed slow cooker.

- Sprinkle soup mix on roast and spoon on soup. Place potatoes around roast.

- Cover and cook on low for 7 to 8 hours or on high for 4 hours. Serves 6 to 8.

Mushroom Beef

3 280-g (10-ounce) can of creamy mushroom soup
⅓ cup (40 g) seasoned breadcrumbs
30 g (1 ounce) French onion soup mix
1.1 kg (2½ pounds) lean beef stew meat
Noodles, cooked

- Combine soups, ½ teaspoon pepper, soup mix, breadcrumbs and ¾ cup (175 ml) water in 6-L (6-quart) slow cooker. Stir in beef cubes and mix well.

- Cover and cook on low for 8 to 9 hours.

- Serve over noodles. Serves 6 to 8.

Beef Roast

1.8 kg (4 pounds) boneless
   rump roast
½ cup (60 g) flour
30 g (1 ounce) brown gravy mix
30 g (1 ounce) French
   onion soup mix

- Cut roast in half (if needed to fit into cooker).

- Place roast in sprayed 5 to 6-L (5 to 6-quart) slow cooker and rub half of flour over roast.

- Combine remaining flour, gravy mix and soup mix in small bowl, gradually add 2 cups (500 ml) water and stir until they mix well. Pour over roast.

- Cover and cook on low for 7 to 8 hours or until roast is tender. Serves 6 to 8.

TIP: This is a great gravy to serve over mashed potatoes or you can use instant mashed potatoes. They will never know the difference and will love the meal!

Smoked Brisket

**1.8–2.7 kg (4–6 pounds)
trimmed brisket
1 285-g (10-ounce) bottle
barbecue sauce
Garlic salt
Celery salt
Worcestershire sauce
1 onion, chopped**

- Place brisket in large shallow dish and pour about half barbecue sauce over top.

- Sprinkle with garlic salt and celery salt. Cover and refrigerate overnight.

- Before cooking, drain marinade and douse brisket with Worcestershire sauce.

- Place chopped onion in slow cooker and place brisket on top of onion.

- Cover and cook on low for 7 to 9 hours.

- With 1 hour left on cooking time, pour remaining barbecue sauce over brisket and cook for an additional 1 hour. Serves 6 to 8.

Good Brisket

½ cup (110 g) brown sugar
1 tablespoon (15 ml) Cajun
  seasoning
2 teaspoons lemon pepper
1 tablespoon (15 ml)
  Worcestershire sauce
1.4–1.8 kg (3–4 pounds)
  trimmed beef brisket

- Combine brown sugar,
  seasoning, lemon pepper and
  Worcestershire sauce in small
  bowl and spread on brisket.

- Place brisket in sprayed, oval
  slow cooker.

- Cover and cook on low for
  6 to 8 hours. Serves 6 to 8.

Sweet and Savoury Brisket

1.4–1.8 kg (3–4 pounds) trimmed
  beef brisket, halved
⅓ cup (110 g) grape or plum
  jam
1 cup (270 g) tomato sauce
30 g (1 ounce) dry onion
  soup mix

- Place half of brisket in
  slow cooker.

- Combine jam, tomato sauce,
  onion soup mix and ¾ teaspoon
  pepper in saucepan and heat just
  enough to mix well. Spread half
  over brisket.

- Top with remaining brisket and
  jam-soup mixture.

- Cover and cook on low for
  8 to 9 hours. Slice brisket and
  serve with cooking juices.
  Serves 6 to 8.

Meat and Potatoes

**4 medium potatoes,
  peeled, sliced**
**570 g (1¼ pounds) lean minced
  beef, browned**
1 onion, sliced
**1 280-g (10-ounce) can cream
  of mushroom soup**
**1 280-g (10-ounce) can
  vegetable beef soup**

- Layer all ingredients with a little salt and pepper in large slow cooker.

- Cover and cook on low for 5 to 6 hours. Serves 4 to 6.

Beef Ribs and Gravy

1.8 kg (4 pounds) beef short ribs
1 onion, sliced
340 g (12 ounces) beef gravy
30 g (1 ounce) beef gravy mix

- Place beef ribs in sprayed 6-L (6-quart) slow cooker. Cover with onion and sprinkle with 1 teaspoon pepper.

- Combine beef gravy and dry gravy mix in small bowl and pour over ribs and onion.

- Cover and cook on low for 9 to 11 hours. (The ribs must cook this long on low to tenderise.) Serves 4 to 6.

*TIP: Serve with hot mashed
  potatoes and gravy.*

Brisket and Gravy

1.4–1.8 kg (3–4 pounds)
    trimmed beef brisket
¼ cup (70 g) chilli sauce
30 g (1 ounce) instant spring
    vegetable soup mix
2 tablespoons (30 ml)
    Worcestershire sauce
3 tablespoons (25 g) cornflour
Mashed potatoes

- Place beef brisket in sprayed 5 to 6-L (5 to 6-quart) slow cooker. Cut to fit if necessary.

- Combine chilli sauce, soup mix, Worcestershire sauce and 1½ cups (375 ml) water in bowl and pour over brisket.

- Cover and cook on low for 9 to 11 hours.

- Remove brisket and keep warm. Pour juices into 2-cup (500-ml) glass measuring cup and skim fat.

- Combine cornflour and ¼ cup (60 ml) water in saucepan. Add 1½ cups (375 ml) juices and cook, while stirring constantly, until gravy thickens.

- Slice beef thinly across grain and serve with mashed potatoes and gravy. Serves 6 to 8.

Shredded Brisket for Sandwiches

2 teaspoons onion powder
1 teaspoon minced garlic
1.4–1.8 kg (3–4 pounds)
  beef brisket
1 tablespoon (15 ml) barbecue
  marinade
1 455-g (16-ounce) bottle
  barbecue sauce
Vienna rolls or
  hamburger buns

- Combine onion powder, minced garlic and marinade in bowl and rub over brisket.

- Place brisket in large, sprayed slow cooker. Add ⅓ cup (75 ml) water to cooker.

- Cover and cook on low for 6 to 8 hours or until brisket is tender.

- Remove brisket, cool and reserve ½ cup (125 ml) cooking juices.

- Shred brisket with 2 forks and place in large saucepan. Add ½ cup (125 ml) cooking juices and barbecue sauce and heat thoroughly.

- Make sandwiches with Vienna rolls or hamburger buns. Serves 6 to 8.

The Best Ever Brisket

1.4–1.8 kg (3–4 pounds) fresh, trimmed brisket
3 onions, sliced
230 g (8 ounces) fresh mushrooms, halved
1 teaspoon seasoned salt
340-g (12 ounces) beer (not light)
1 cup (270 g) chilli sauce
2 green chillies, chopped

- If necessary, trim brisket to fit into large, sprayed oval slow cooker. Layer onions and mushrooms in bottom of slow cooker and sprinkle with seasoned salt. Top with brisket.

- Combine beer, chilli sauce and green chillies in medium bowl and mix well. Pour mixture over brisket in slow cooker.

- Cover and cook on low heat for 10 to 12 hours or on high for 5 to 6 hours. When ready to serve, remove brisket from slow cooker and thinly slice meat across the grain.

- Place brisket on serving platter and place onions and mushrooms on top of brisket. Serves 8 to 10.

A Different Corned Beef

2 onions, sliced
Lemon pepper
1.4–1.8 kg (3–4 pounds)
seasoned corned beef
¼ cup (85 g) honey
¼ cup (60 ml) orange
juice concentrate
1 tablespoon (15 ml) mustard

- Place sliced onions in large slow cooker. Add 1 cup (250 ml) water. Sprinkle lemon pepper liberally over corned beef and place on top of onion. Cover and cook on low for 7 to 9 hours.

- Remove corned beef from slow cooker and place in ovenproof pan. Preheat oven to 190° C (375° F).

- Combine honey, juice and mustard and spoon over corned beef. Bake for 30 minutes and baste occasionally with glaze before serving. Serves 6 to 8.

Justice with Short Ribs

Flour
1.4 kg (3 pounds) beef short ribs
3 tablespoons (45 ml) olive oil
1 onion, thinly sliced
½ cup (135 g) chilli sauce
¼ cup (55 g) brown sugar
3 tablespoons (45 ml) vinegar
½ teaspoon mustard
1 teaspoon chilli powder
2 tablespoons (15 g) flour

- Coat ribs with lots of salt and pepper; then dredge in flour, coating well. Brown short ribs in oil in large frypan over medium-high heat until they are light brown.

- Place onion, chilli sauce, brown sugar, vinegar, mustard and chilli powder in sprayed slow cooker; mix thoroughly.

- Place browned ribs into slow cooker. Cover and cook on low for 6 to 8 hours.

- Remove ribs to serving platter and turn slow cooker to high heat. Combine 2 tablespoons flour with ¾ cup (175 ml) water in bowl and stir into sauce in slow cooker.

- Cook for 10 minutes or until mixture thickens. When serving, spoon sauce over ribs. Serves 6.

Beef and Pasta al Grande

680 g (1½ pounds) lean
  minced beef
1 chopped onion
1 chopped red capsicum
1 chopped green capsicum
455 g (16 ounces) cheddar
  cheese, cubed
2 425-g (15-ounce) cans
  stewed tomatoes
  with liquid
2 425-g (15-ounce) cans
  corn kernels, drained
230 g (8 ounces) fettuccini
  (medium egg noodles)
1 cup (115 g) shredded
  cheddar cheese
Fresh parsley or
  spring onions

- Brown ground beef in frypan and drain fat.

- Place beef in sprayed 5 to 6-L (5 to 6-quart) slow cooker, add onions and capsicums, cheese cubes, tomatoes, corn and about 1 teaspoon salt and mix well.

- Cover and cook on low for 4 to 5 hours.

- Cook noodles according to package directions, drain and fold into beef-tomato mixture. Cook for an additional 30 minutes to heat thoroughly.

- When ready to serve, top with cheddar cheese, several sprinkles of chopped fresh parsley or chopped fresh spring onions. Serves 4 to 6.

Sauce for Fancy Meatballs

1 455-g (16-ounce) can
    whole-berry
    cranberry sauce
1 cup (270 g) tomato sauce
⅔ cup (150 g) brown sugar
½ cup (125 ml) beef stock
510 g (18 ounces) frozen
    meatballs, thawed

- Combine cranberry sauce,
  tomato sauce, brown sugar and
  stock in large slow cooker.

- Turn heat to high and let mixture
  come to a boil for 30 minutes to
  1 hour. Place package of thawed
  meatballs in sauce.

- Cover and cook on low for
  2 hours.

- Remove meatballs to serving
  dish with slotted spoon. Insert
  toothpicks for easy pick up.

- Serve as an appetiser, for
  dinner or as part of a buffet.
  Serves 4 to 6.

Southwest Spaghetti

680 g (1½ pounds) minced
    lean beef
2½ teaspoons chilli powder
1 425-g (15-ounce) can tomato
    soup
200 g (7 ounces) spaghetti
1 heaped tablespoon (15 ml)
    steak seasoning
Shredded cheddar cheese

- Brown beef in frypan until
  no longer pink. Place in
  4 to 5-L (4 to 5-quart)
  slow cooker.

- Add chilli powder, tomato soup,
  spaghetti, 2⅓ cups (575 ml)
  water and steak seasoning and
  mix well.

- Cover and cook on low for
  6 to 7 hours.

- When ready to serve, cover with
  lots of shredded cheddar cheese.
  Serves 4 to 6.

Stuffed Cabbage

10–12 large cabbage leaves
680 g (1½ pounds) lean minced
beef
½ cup (95 g) brown rice
1 egg, beaten
¼ teaspoon ground cinnamon
1 425-g (15-ounce) can tomato
soup

- Wash cabbage leaves, place in saucepan of boiling water and turn off heat. Soak for about 5 minutes.

- Remove leaves, drain and cool.

- Combine beef, rice, egg, 1 teaspoon salt, ½ teaspoon pepper and cinnamon in bowl and mix well.

- Place 2 tablespoons (30 ml) beef mixture on each cabbage leaf and roll tightly. (If you can't get 10 to 12 large leaves, put 2 together to make 1 large leaf.)

- Stack rolls in sprayed, oval slow cooker and pour tomato sauce over rolls.

- Cover and cook on high for 1 hour, lower heat to low and cook for an additional 6 to 7 hours. Serves 4 to 6.

Make-Believe Lasagna

455 g (1 pound) lean minced
  beef
1 onion, chopped
½ teaspoon garlic powder
1 510-g (18-ounce) can
  spaghetti sauce
½ teaspoon ground oregano
6–8 lasagna sheets
340 g (12 ounces) cottage cheese
½ cup (50 g) grated parmesan
  cheese
340 g (12 ounces) shredded
  mozzarella cheese

- Brown beef and onion
  in large frypan. Add garlic
  powder, spaghetti sauce and
  oregano. Cook just until
  thoroughly warm.

- Spoon layer of meat sauce in
  sprayed, oval slow cooker. Add
  layer lasagna sheets (break to fit
  slow cooker).

- Top with layer of half remaining
  meat sauce, half cottage cheese,
  half parmesan cheese and half
  mozzarella cheese. Repeat
  layers and start with more
  lasagna sheets.

- Cover and cook on low for
  6 to 8 hours. Serves 4 to 6.

Mac 'n Cheese Supper

680 g (1½ pounds) lean minced beef
400 g (14 ounces) macaroni and cheese dinners
1 425-g (15-ounce) can corn kernels, drained
1½ cups (170 g) shredded Colby cheese

- Sprinkle beef with ½ teaspoon salt, brown in skillet until no longer pink and drain.

- Prepare pasta and cheese according to package directions.

- Spoon in beef, pasta and corn in sprayed 5-L (5-quart) slow cooker and mix well.

- Cover and cook on low for 4 to 5 hours.

- When ready to serve, sprinkle cheese over top and leave in cooker until cheese melts. Serves 4 to 6.

Meat on
the Table

**680–910 g (1½–2 pounds)
lean minced beef
30 g (1 ounce) French
onion soup mix
⅔ cup (55 g) quick-cooking
oats
2 eggs
1 340-g (12-ounce) bottle
chilli sauce**

- Combine beef, onion soup mix, oats, eggs, ¾ cup (204 g) chilli sauce and 1 teaspoon (5 ml) black pepper in bowl and mix well.

- Shape meat mixture into round ball, place in sprayed slow cooker and pat down into loaf shape.

- Cover and cook on low for 3 to 4 hours.

- Before last half hour of cooking time, spread remaining chilli sauce over top of loaf and continue cooking.

- Use foil handles to lift meat loaf out of slow cooker. Serves 4 to 6.

Jack's Meat Loaf

**910 g (2 pounds) lean minced
  beef**
2 eggs
½ cup (135 g) chilli sauce
**1¼ cups (150 g) seasoned
  breadcrumbs**
**230 g (8 ounces) shredded Colby
  cheese**

- Combine beef, eggs, chilli sauce
  and breadcrumbs in bowl and
  mix well.

- Shape half beef mixture into flat
  loaf and place in sprayed
  slow cooker.

- Sprinkle half cheese over meat
  loaf and press into meat.

- Form remaining meat mixture in
  same shape as first layer, place
  over cheese and seal seams.

- Cover and cook on low for
  6 to 7 hours.

- When ready to serve, sprinkle
  remaining cheese over loaf
  and leave in cooker until
  cheese melts.

- Carefully remove loaf with foil
  handles and place on serving
  plate. Serves 4 to 6.

Hash Brown Dinner

680 g (1½ pounds) lean minced chuck, browned
30 g (1 ounce) brown gravy mix
425-g (15-ounce) can creamed corn
425-g (15-ounce) can corn kernels
230 g (8 ounces) shredded cheddar cheese
510 g (18 ounces) frozen hash browns, partially thawed
280-g (10-ounce) can mushroom soup
1 145-g (5-ounce) can evaporated milk

- Place browned beef in sprayed slow cooker and toss with dry brown gravy.

- Add creamed corn and corn and cover with half cheddar cheese.

- Top with hash browns and remaining cheese.

- Combine mushroom soup and evaporated milk in bowl. Mix well and pour over hash browns and cheese.

- Cover and cook on low for 6 to 8 hours. Serves 4 to 6.

Fiesta Beef and Rice

680 g (1½ pounds) lean minced beef
1 425-g (15-ounce) can stewed tomatoes
200 g (7 ounces) beef-flavoured rice mix
1 310-g (11-ounce) can corn kernels, drained
Salsa

- Sprinkle salt and pepper over beef and shape into small patties.

- Place in sprayed 5-L (5-quart) oval slow cooker.

- Combine stewed tomatoes, rice, corn and 2 cups (500 ml) water in bowl and mix well. Spoon over beef patties.

- Cover and cook on low for 4 to 5 hours.

- When ready to serve, place large spoonful of salsa on each serving. Serves 4 to 6.

Cowboy Feed

680 g (1½ pounds) lean
    minced beef
2 onions, coarsely
    chopped
5 medium potatoes,
    peeled, sliced
1 425-g (15-ounce) can kidney
    beans, rinsed, drained
1 425-g (15-ounce) can borlotti
    beans, drained
1 425-g (15-ounce) can
    stewed tomatoes
1 280-g (10-ounce) can tomato
    soup
½ teaspoon basil
½ teaspoon oregano
2 teaspoons minced garlic

- Sprinkle beef with some salt and pepper, brown in frypan and drain.

- Place onions in slow cooker and spoon beef over onions.

- On top of beef, layer potatoes, kidney and borlotti beans.

- Pour stewed tomatoes and tomato soup over beans and potatoes and sprinkle with basil, oregano and garlic.

- Cover and cook on low for 7 to 8 hours. Serves 4 to 6.

Cheeseburger Dinner

3 medium potatoes, sliced
40 g scalloped potato mix
1 tablespoon bacon bits
⅓ cup (75 ml) milk
¼ cup (60 g) butter, melted
680 g (1½ pounds) lean minced beef
1 onion, coarsely chopped
Canola oil
425-g (15-ounce) can corn kernels with liquid
230 g (8 ounces) shredded cheddar cheese

- Place potatoes, scalloped potato mix and bacon in sprayed slow cooker.

- Pour 2¼ cups (560 ml) boiling water, milk and butter over potatoes.

- Brown beef and onion in little oil in frypan, drain and spoon over potatoes. Top with corn.

- Cover and cook on low for 6 to 7 hours.

- When ready to serve, sprinkle cheese over corn. Serves 4 to 6.

Beef and Macaroni Dinner

280 g (10 ounces) macaroni, cooked, drained
3 tablespoons (45 ml) canola oil
680 g (1½ pounds) lean minced beef, browned, drained
1 onion, chopped
3 sticks celery, chopped
2 280-g (10-ounce) cans tomato soup
170-g (6-ounce) can tomato paste
1 beef stock cube
230 g (8 ounces) cubed cheddar cheese

- Toss cooked pasta with oil to make sure pasta does not stick together.

- Place in sprayed slow cooker.

- Add beef, onion, celery, tomato soup, tomato paste, beef stock cube and ⅔ cup (150 ml) water and stir to mix well.

- Cover and cook on low for 4 to 6 hours. Before last hour of cooking time, stir in cubed cheese. Serves 4 to 6.

Beef-Bean Medley

455 g (1 pound) lean minced beef
1 onion, chopped
6 slices bacon, cooked, crumbled
2 425-g (15-ounce) cans baked beans with ham sauce
1 425-g (15-ounce) can butter beans, rinsed, drained
1 425-g (15-ounce) can kidney beans, rinsed, drained
½ cup (135 g) tomato sauce
½ cup (110 g) brown sugar
3 tablespoons (45 ml) vinegar
370 g (13 ounces) original corn chips
230 g (8 ounces) shredded cheddar cheese

- Brown beef and onion in frypan, drain and transfer to sprayed 4 to 5-L (4 to 5-quart) slow cooker.

- Add bacon and all 4 cans of beans.

- Combine tomato sauce, brown sugar and vinegar in bowl. Add to cooker and stir.

- Cover and cook on low for 4 to 6 hours.

- When ready to serve, spoon over corn chips and sprinkle cheese over top. Serves 4 to 6.

Abundant Stuffed Shells

20–22 jumbo pasta shells
340 g (¾ pound) lean minced
**   beef, browned, drained**
½ cup (80 g) finely chopped
**   onion**
1 cup (115 g) shredded
**   cheddar cheese**
⅓ cup (40 g) seasoned
**   breadcrumbs**
1 teaspoon minced garlic
½ teaspoon Italian seasoning
1 egg, beaten
2 740-g (26-ounce) jar
**   spaghetti sauce**
½ cup (60 g) shredded
**   mozzarella cheese**

- Cook pasta shells for 7 minutes in boiling water in saucepan (they need only to be partially cooked), drain and place on sheet of wax paper.

- Combine beef, onion, cheddar cheese, breadcrumbs, garlic, seasoning and egg in bowl. Carefully stuff partially cooked pasta shells with spoonful of meat mixture.

- Pour 1 jar spaghetti sauce in sprayed slow cooker. Transfer stuffed shells on top of sauce. Pour remaining sauce evenly over pasta. Sprinkle with mozzarella cheese.

- Cover and cook on low heat 4 to 5 hours. Do not over cook. Serves 4 to 6.

Italy's Best

**910 g (2 pounds) lean minced
  beef**
1 large onion, chopped
**1 green capsicum,
  seeded, chopped**
1 teaspoon minced garlic
**1 425-g (15-ounce) can
  tomato soup**
**1 425-g (15-ounce) can Italian
  stewed tomatoes**
2 teaspoons Italian seasoning
455 g (16 ounces) penne pasta
**280 g (10 ounces) frozen, chopped
  spinach, thawed**
**340 g (12 ounces) shredded
  mozzarella cheese**

- Brown and cook beef, onion,
  capsicum and garlic in large
  frypan for about 15 minutes.
  Drain and place mixture in
  sprayed slow cooker.

- Stir in tomato soup, stewed
  tomatoes, Italian seasoning and
  a little salt and pepper.
  Cover and cook on low for
  7 to 8 hours or on high for
  3 hours 30 minutes.

- Cook pasta according to package
  directions and drain.

- Last 30 minutes of cooking time,
  turn heat to high (if cooking on
  low) stir in pasta, spinach and
  cheese and continue cooking.
  Serves 6 to 8.

Italian Tortellini

230 g (½ pound) minced round
   steak
455 g (1 pound) bulk
   Italian sausage meat
1 425-g (15-ounce) jar
   tomato pasta sauce
1 425-g (15-ounce) can Italian
   stewed tomatoes with
   liquid
1½ cups (110 g) sliced fresh
   mushrooms
255 g (9 ounces) refrigerated
   cheese-filled tortellini
1½ cups (170 g) shredded
   mozzarella cheese

- Brown and cook beef and
  sausage in large frypan for
  about 10 minutes on medium-
  low heat and drain.

- Combine meat mixture, pasta
  sauce, tomatoes and mushrooms
  in 4 to 5-L (4 to 5-quart)
  slow cooker.

- Cover and cook on low
  6 to 8 hours.

- Stir in pasta and sprinkle with
  mozzarella cheese.

- Turn cooker to high and
  continue cooking for an
  additional 10 to 15 minutes or
  until pasta is tender.
  Serves 4 to 6.

Sloppy Joes

1.4 kg (3 pounds) minced beef
1 tablespoon (15 ml) minced
**   garlic**
1 large onion, finely
**   chopped**
2 sticks celery, chopped
¼ cup (55 g) brown sugar
3½ tablespoons (55 g) mustard
1 tablespoon (15 ml) chilli
**   powder**
1½ cups (410 g) tomato sauce
3 tablespoons (45 ml)
**   Worcestershire sauce**

- Brown beef, garlic and onion in very large frypan and drain.

- Combine celery, brown sugar, mustard, chilli powder, tomato sauce and Worcestershire sauce in sprayed 5-L (5-quart) slow cooker. Stir in meat mixture.

- Cover and cook on low heat for 6 to 7 hours. Serves 6 to 8.

TIP: This will make enough to fill 16 to 18 hamburger buns.

Beef and Gravy

910 g (2 pounds) sirloin steak or
**   thick round steak**
Canola oil
30 g (1 ounce) onion
**   soup mix**
1 280-g (10-ounce) can
**   mushroom soup**
1 115-g (4-ounce) can sliced
**   mushrooms, drained**
Noodles, cooked

- Cut steak in 1.2-cm (½-inch) pieces. Brown beef in frypan in a little oil and place in 5 to 6-L (5 to 6-quart) slow cooker.

- Combine onion soup mix, mushroom soup, mushrooms and ½ cup (125 ml) water in bowl and mix well. Spoon over top of beef.

- Cover and cook on low for 7 to 8 hours. Serve over noodles. Serves 4 to 6.

Special Hot Dog Dinner

455 g (1 pound) beef wieners
2 425-g (15-ounce) bottles
   chunky vegetable
   pasta sauce
1 onion, finely chopped
1 280-g (10-ounce) can
   cream of celery soup
½ can milk
½ cup cheddar cheese, cubed
2 chopped green chillies
Corn chips

- Cut wieners in 1.2-cm (½-inch) pieces and place in sprayed slow cooker.

- Combine chilli, onion, soup, milk, cheese and green chillies in saucepan. (Omit green chillies if serving to kids.)

- Heat just enough to mix ingredients well. Spoon over wieners.

- Cover and cook on low for 1 hour 30 minutes to 2 hours.

- Serve over bowl of small corn chips slightly crushed. Serves 4 to 6.

Chicken & Turkey

Honey-Baked, Oranged & Noodled

Chicken & Turkey Contents

Chicken & Turkey Contents

Chicken Olé

6 boneless, skinless chicken
    breast halves
230 g (8 ounces)
    cream cheese, softened
1 455-g (16-ounce) jar salsa
2 teaspoons cumin
1 bunch fresh spring
    onions with tops,
    chopped

- Pound chicken breasts to flatten. Beat cream cheese in bowl until smooth, add salsa, cumin and onions and mix gently.

- Place heaped spoonfuls of cream cheese mixture on each chicken breast and roll. (There will be leftover cream cheese mixture.)

- Place chicken breast seam side down in sprayed slow cooker. Spoon remaining cream cheese mixture over each chicken roll.

- Cover and cook on low for 5 to 6 hours. Serves 4 to 6.

Chicken for the Gods

1¾ cups (180 g) flour
2 tablespoons (30 ml)
    mustard
6 boneless, skinless
    chicken breast halves
2 tablespoons (30 ml) canola oil
1 280-g (10-ounce) can
    chicken soup

- Place flour and mustard in shallow bowl and dredge chicken to coat all sides.

- Brown chicken breasts in oil in frypan. Place all breasts in 6-L (6-quart) oval slow cooker.

- Pour chicken soup over chicken and add about ¼ cup (60 ml) water.

- Cover and cook on low for 6 to 7 hours. Serves 4 to 6.

Apricot Chicken

6 boneless, skinless
   chicken breast halves
1 340-g (12-ounce) jar
   apricot jam
1 230-g (8-ounce) bottle
   Italian dressing
30 g (1 ounce) onion
   soup mix

- Place chicken in sprayed
  6-L (6-quart) slow cooker.

- Combine apricot jam, Italian
  dressing, onion soup mix and ¼
  cup (60 ml) water and stir well.
  Cover chicken breasts
  with sauce mixture.

- Cover and cook on low for
  5 to 6 hours. Serves 4 to 6.

Asparagus-Rice Chicken

1¼ cups (250 g) converted rice
680 g (2 pounds) boneless,
   skinless chicken
   breast halves
Dried parsley
2 chicken stock cubes
1 400-g (14-ounce) can
   cream of asparagus soup

- Place rice in lightly sprayed
  slow cooker. Cut chicken into
  slices and place over rice.

- Sprinkle with parsley and a
  little pepper.

- Combine soup, chicken stock
  cubes and 1 cup (250 ml) water
  in saucepan. Heat just enough to
  mix well. Pour over chicken and
  rice.

- Cover and cook on low for
  6 to 8 hours. Serves 4 to 6.

Artichoke-Chicken Pasta

680 g (1½ pounds) boneless, skinless chicken breast tenders
1 425-g (15-ounce) can artichoke hearts, quartered
¾ cup (110 g) chopped, roasted red capsicum
230 g (8 ounces) Colby cheese, shredded
1 tablespoon (15 ml) Worcestershire sauce
1 280-g (10-ounce) can cream of chicken soup
230 g (8 ounces) shredded cheddar cheese
4 cups (300 g) hot, cooked bow-tie pasta

- Combine chicken, artichoke, roasted capsicums, Colby cheese, Worcestershire sauce and soup in slow cooker and mix well.

- Cover and cook on low for 6 to 8 hours. About 20 minutes before serving, fold in cheddar cheese, hot pasta and a little salt and pepper. Serves 4.

Chicken Curry over Rice

3 large boneless, skinless chicken
   breast halves
½ cup (125 ml) chicken stock
1 280-g (10-ounce) can cream of
   chicken soup
1 onion, coarsely chopped
1 red capsicum, seeded, julienned
¼ cup (40 g) golden raisins
1½ teaspoons curry powder
¼ teaspoon ground ginger
Rice, cooked

- Cut chicken into thin strips and place in sprayed 5 to 6-L (5 to 6-quart) slow cooker.

- Combine stock, soup, onion, capsicum, raisins, curry powder and ginger in bowl and mix well. Pour over chicken.

- Cover and cook on low for 3 to 4 hours. Serve over rice. Serves 4.

Bacon-Wrapped Chicken

70 g (2.5 ounces) beef jerky
6 boneless, skinless
   chicken breast
   halves
6 slices bacon
2 280-g (10-ounce) cans
   mushroom soup
170 g (6 ounces) instant
   chicken-flavoured
   rice, cooked

- Place beef jerky sliced in 5-L (5-quart) slow cooker.

- Roll each chicken breast half in slice of bacon and place over beef jerky.

- Heat soup and ⅓ cup (75 ml) water in saucepan just enough to mix well and pour over chicken.

- Cover and cook on low for 7 to 8 hours.

- Serve over rice. Serves 4 to 6.

Broccoli-Cheese Chicken

4 boneless, skinless
  chicken breast
  halves
2 tablespoons (30 g) butter,
  melted
1 280-g (10-ounce) can
  cream of celery soup
125 g (4 ounces) cream cheese
¼ cup (60 ml) milk
280 g (10 ounces) frozen
  broccoli florets
Rice, cooked

- Dry chicken with paper towels
  and place in sprayed, oval slow
  cooker.

- Combine melted butter, soup,
  cheese and milk in bowl and
  spoon over chicken. Cover and
  cook on low for 4 to 6 hours.

- Remove cooker lid and place
  broccoli over chicken. Cover
  and cook for an additional
  1 hour. Serve over rice.
  Serves 4.

Cream Cheese Chicken

4 boneless, skinless
  chicken breast
  halves
2 tablespoons (30 g) butter,
  melted
1 280-g (10-ounce) can cream
  of mushroom soup
2 tablespoons (30 ml) Italian
  seasoning
½ cup (125 ml) sherry
230 g (8 ounces) cream
  cheese, cubed
Noodles, cooked

- Wash chicken, dry with paper
  towels and brush melted butter
  over chicken.

- Place in sprayed, oval
  slow cooker and add
  remaining ingredients.

- Cover and cook on low for
  6 to 7 hours. Serve over noodles.
  Serves 4.

Chicken and Noodles

910 g (2 pounds) boneless, skinless chicken breast halves
¼ cup (30 g) cornflour
⅓ cup (75 ml) soy sauce
2 onions, chopped
3 sticks celery, sliced diagonally
1 red capsicum, seeded, julienned
2 400-g (14-ounce) cans mixed Chinese vegetables, drained
¼ cup (60 ml) treacle
Chow mein noodles

- Place chicken and 2 cups (500 ml) water in sprayed slow cooker.

- Cover and cook on low for 3 to 4 hours. At least 1 hour before serving, remove chicken and cut into bite-size pieces.

- Combine cornflour and soy sauce in bowl and mix well. Stir into slow cooker. Add onions, celery, capsicum, mixed vegetables and treacle. Cover and cook on high heat for 1 to 2 hours.

- Serve over noodles. Serves 4 to 6.

Chicken and Pasta

455 g (16 ounces)
    frozen whole green
    beans, thawed
1 onion, chopped
1 cup (70 g) fresh mushroom
    halves
3 boneless, skinless
    chicken breast halves
1 425-g (15-ounce) can Italian
    stewed tomatoes
1 chicken stock cube
1 teaspoon minced garlic
1 teaspoon Italian seasoning
230 g (8 ounces) fettuccini
    (medium egg noodles)
115 g (4 ounces) grated
    parmesan cheese

- Place green beans, onion and mushrooms in sprayed 4-L (4-quart) slow cooker.

- Cut chicken into 2.5-cm (1-inch) pieces and place over vegetables.

- Combine stewed tomatoes, chicken stock cube, garlic and Italian seasoning in small bowl. Pour over chicken.

- Cover and cook on low for 5 to 6 hours.

- Cook pasta according to package directions and drain.

- Serve chicken over pasta sprinkled with parmesan cheese. Serves 4.

TIP: Add ¼ cup (60 g) butter to
    give this dish a richer taste.

Chicken and Vegetables

4–5 boneless, skinless chicken breast halves
2 teaspoons seasoned salt
455 g (16 ounces) frozen broccoli florets, cauliflower and carrots, thawed
1 280-g (10-ounce) can cream of celery soup
230 g (8 ounces) shredded cheddar cheese

- Cut chicken into strips, sprinkle with seasoned salt and place in sprayed slow cooker.

- Combine vegetables, celery soup and half cheese in large bowl and mix well. Spoon over chicken breasts.

- Cover and cook on low for 4 to 5 hours.

- About 10 minutes before serving, sprinkle remaining cheese on top of casserole. Serves 4 to 6.

Chicken Delicious

**5–6 boneless skinless
  chicken breast halves
455 g (16 ounces) frozen
  broccoli florets, thawed
1 red capsicum, seeded, julienned
455-g (16-ounce) jar three-cheese
  pasta sauce
3 tablespoons (45 ml) sherry
Noodles, cooked**

- Brown chicken in frypan and place in sprayed 5 to 6-L (5 to 6-quart) oval slow cooker.

- Place broccoli on plate, remove much of stem and discard.

- Combine broccoli, capsicum, cheese sauce and sherry in bowl and mix well. Spoon over chicken.

- Cover and cook on low for 4 to 5 hours. Serve over noodles. Serves 4 to 6.

Chicken Delight

¾ cup (150 g) white rice
½ litre carton chicken stock
30 g (1 ounce) onion soup mix
1 red capsicum,
    seeded, chopped
2 280-g (10-ounce) cans
    cream of celery soup
¾ cup (175 ml) white
    cooking wine
4–6 boneless skinless
    chicken breast halves
85 g (3 ounces)
    grated fresh
    parmesan cheese

- Combine rice, stock, soup mix, capsicum, celery soup, ¾ cup (175 ml) water, wine and several sprinkles of black pepper in bowl and mix well. (Make sure to mix soup well with liquids.)

- Place chicken in sprayed 6-L (6-quart) oval slow cooker.

- Pour rice-soup mixture over chicken.

- Cover and cook on low for 4 to 6 hours.

- One hour before serving, sprinkle parmesan cheese over chicken. Serves 4 to 6.

Chicken Dinner

1 cup (200 g) rice
1 tablespoon (15 ml) chicken
   seasoning
30 g (1 ounce) onion
   soup mix
1 green capsicum,
   seeded, chopped
1 diced roasted red pepper
¾ teaspoon (4 ml) dried basil
½ litre carton chicken stock
280-g (10-ounce) can cream
   of chicken soup
5–6 boneless, skinless
   chicken breast halves

- Combine rice, chicken
  seasoning, onion soup mix,
  capsicum, roasted red pepper,
  basil, stock, ½ cup (125 ml)
  water and chicken soup in bowl
  and mix well.

- Place chicken in sprayed, oval
  slow cooker and cover with rice
  mixture.

- Cover and cook on low for
  6 to 7 hours. Serves 4 to 6.

Chicken Ready

6 medium new potatoes
   with peels, quartered
4–5 carrots
4–5 boneless, skinless
   chicken breast halves
1 tablespoon (15 ml)
   chicken seasoning
2 280-g (10-ounce) cans
   cream of chicken soup
⅓ cup (75 ml) white wine or
   cooking wine

- Cut carrots into 1.2-cm
  (½-inch) pieces. Place potatoes
  and carrots in slow cooker.

- Sprinkle chicken with chicken
  seasoning and place over
  vegetables.

- Heat soups, wine and ¼ cup
  (60 ml) water in saucepan just to
  mix and pour over chicken
  and vegetables.

- Cover and cook on low for
  5 to 6 hours. Serves 4 to 5.

Chicken Fajitas

910 g (2 pounds) boneless,
   skinless chicken breast
   halves
1 onion, thinly sliced
1 red capsicum, cored,
   seeded, julienned
1 teaspoon ground cumin
1½ teaspoons chilli powder
1 tablespoon (15 ml) lime juice
½ cup (125 ml) chicken stock
8–10 warm flour tortillas
Guacamole
Sour cream
Lettuce and tomatoes

- Cut chicken into diagonal strips and place in sprayed slow cooker. Top with onion and capsicum.

- Combine cumin, chilli powder, lime juice and chicken stock in bowl and pour over chicken and vegetables.

- Cover and cook on low for 5 to 7 hours.

- Serve several slices of chicken mixture with sauce into centre of each warm tortilla and fold.

- Serve with guacamole, sour cream, lettuce or tomatoes or plain. Serves 4 to 6.

Chicken for Dinner

5–6 boneless, skinless
    chicken breast halves
6 carrots, peeled, cut
    in 2.5-cm (1-inch) lengths
1 425-g (15-ounce) can cut
    green beans, drained
1 425-g (15-ounce) can
    whole new potatoes, drained
2 280-g (10-ounce) cans
    cream of mushroom soup
Shredded cheddar cheese

- Wash, dry chicken with paper towels and place in sprayed, oval slow cooker.

- In bowl, combine carrots, green beans, potatoes and mushroom soup and pour over chicken in cooker.

- Cover and cook on low for 8 to 10 hours.

- When ready to serve, sprinkle cheese over top. Serves 4 to 6.

Chicken-Ready Dinner

170 g (6 ounces) stuffing mix
3 cups (420 g) cooked,
    chopped chicken
    breasts
455 g (16 ounces)
    frozen whole green
    beans, thawed
2 340-g (12-ounce) jars
    chicken sauce

- Prepare stuffing mix according to package directions and place in oval slow cooker.

- Follow with layer of chopped chicken and place green beans over chicken. Pour chicken sauce over green beans.

- Cover and cook on low for 3 hours 30 minutes to 4 hours. Serves 4 to 6.

Chicken Marseilles

4–5 boneless, skinless chicken breast halves
2 tablespoons (30 g) butter
60 g (2 ounces) French onion soup mix
½ teaspoon dill
1 cup (250 ml) milk
Brown rice, cooked
¾ cup (180 g) sour cream

- Place chicken in large, sprayed slow cooker.

- Combine butter, onion soup mix, dill, milk and ½ cup (125 ml) water in saucepan and heat just enough for butter to melt and ingredients to mix well. Pour over chicken.

- Cover and cook on low for 3 to 5 hours.

- When ready to serve, remove chicken to platter with hot, cooked brown rice and cover to keep warm.

- Add sour cream to cooker liquid and stir well. Pour sauce over chicken and rice. Serves 4 to 5.

Chicken Breast Deluxe

4 slices bacon
5–6 boneless, skinless
   chicken breast halves
1 cup (100 g) sliced celery
1 cup (90 g) sliced red capsicum
1 280-g (10-ounce) can
   cream of chicken soup
2 tablespoons (30 ml) white
   wine or cooking wine
6 slices Swiss cheese
2 tablespoons (30 ml) dried
   parsley

- Cook bacon in large frypan, drain, crumble and reserve drippings. Place chicken in frypan with bacon drippings and lightly brown on both sides.

- Transfer chicken to sprayed, oval slow cooker and place celery and capsicum over chicken.

- In same frypan, combine soup and wine, stir and spoon over vegetables and chicken. Cover and cook on low for 3 to 4 hours.

- Top with slices of cheese over each chicken breast and add parsley. Cook for additional 10 minutes.

- Serve with creamy sauce and sprinkle with crumbled bacon. Serves 4 to 6.

Chicken Strips

**5 boneless, skinless chicken
    breast halves
1 455-g (16-ounce) jar alfredo
    sauce
455 g (16 ounces) frozen
    green peas, thawed
1½ cups (170 g) shredded
    mozzarella cheese
Noodles, cooked**

- Cut chicken into strips and place in sprayed slow cooker.

- Combine alfredo sauce, peas and cheese in bowl and mix well. Spoon over chicken strips.

- Cover and cook on low for 5 to 6 hours.

- When ready to serve, spoon over noodles. Serves 4 to 5.

*TIP: Use 1 (10 ounce/280 g) can
    chicken soup and
    1 (10 ounce/280 g) can
    mushroom soup for a
    tasty change.*

Chow Mein Chicken

4 boneless, skinless
    chicken breast halves
2–3 cups (200–300 g)
    sliced celery
1 onion, coarsely chopped
⅓ cup (75 ml) soy sauce
¼ teaspoon cayenne pepper
½ litre carton chicken stock
1 425-g (15-ounce) can bean
    sprouts, drained
1 230-g (8-ounce) can water
    chestnuts, drained
1 170-g (6-ounce) can
    bamboo shoots
¼ cup (30 g) flour
Chow mein noodles

- Combine chicken, celery, onion, soy sauce, cayenne pepper and chicken stock in sprayed slow cooker. Cover and cook on low for 3 to 4 hours.

- Add bean sprouts, water chestnuts and bamboo shoots to chicken. Mix flour and ¼ cup (60 ml) water in bowl and stir into chicken and vegetables.

- Cook for an additional 1 hour. Serve over noodles. Serves 4.

Classy Chicken Dinner

170 g (6 ounces) instant
  chicken-flavoured rice
1 455-g (16-ounce) jar
  three-cheese sauce
12–15 frozen chicken
  breast tenderloins,
  thawed
1 cup (145 g) frozen baby
  green peas, thawed

- Pour 2½ cups (625 ml) water,
  rice and seasoning packet in
  sprayed 5-L (5-quart) slow
  cooker and stir well.

- Spoon in cheese sauce and mix
  well. Place chicken in slow
  cooker and cover with green
  peas.

- Cover and cook on low for
  4 to 5 hours. Serves 4.

Creamy Chicken and Potatoes

4 boneless, skinless
  chicken breast halves
2 teaspoons chicken seasoning
8–10 small new (red)
  potatoes with peels
1 280-g (10-ounce) can cream of
  chicken soup
230 g (8 ounces) sour cream

- Sprinkle chicken breasts with
  chicken seasoning and place
  in slow cooker.

- Arrange new potatoes
  around chicken.

- Combine soup, sour cream
  and good amount of black
  pepper in bowl. Spoon over
  chicken.

- Cover and cook on low for
  4 to 6 hours. Serves 4.

Creamed Chicken

**4 large boneless, skinless
  chicken breast halves**
Lemon juice
1 red capsicum, seeded, chopped
**2 sticks celery, sliced
  diagonally**
**1 280-g (10-ounce) can cream
  of chicken soup**
**1 280-g (10-ounce) can cream
  of celery soup**
⅓ cup (75 ml) dry white wine
**115 g (4 ounces) grated
  parmesan cheese**
Rice, cooked

- Wash and pat chicken dry with paper towels, rub a little lemon juice over chicken and sprinkle with a little salt and pepper.

- Place in sprayed slow cooker and top with celery.

- Combine soups and wine in saucepan and heat just enough to mix thoroughly.

- Pour over chicken and sprinkle with parmesan cheese.

- Cover and cook on low for 6 to 7 hours.

- Serve over rice. Serves 4 to 5.

Creamed Chicken and Vegetables

4 large boneless, skinless chicken breast halves
1 280-g (10-ounce) can cream of chicken soup
1 455-g (16-ounce) package frozen peas and carrots, thawed
1 340-g (12-ounce) jar chicken sauce
Thick-sliced bread

- Cut chicken in thin slices.

- Pour soup and ½ cup (125 ml) water into sprayed 6-L (6-quart) slow cooker, mix and add chicken slices.

- Sprinkle a little salt and lots of pepper over chicken and soup.

- Cover and cook on low for 4 to 5 hours.

- Add peas and carrots, chicken sauce and ½ cup (125 ml) water. Increase heat to high and cook for about 1 hour or until peas and carrots are tender.

- Serve over thick slices of bread. Serves 4.

Creamy Salsa Chicken

4–5 boneless, skinless
  chicken breast halves
30 g (1 ounce) dry taco
  seasoning mix
1 cup (265 g) salsa
½ cup (120 g) sour cream

- Place chicken in sprayed 5 to
  6-L (5 to 6-quart) slow cooker
  and add ¼ cup (60 ml) water.

- Sprinkle taco seasoning mix
  over chicken and top with salsa.

- Cover and cook on low for
  5 to 6 hours.

- When ready to serve, remove
  chicken and place on platter.
  Stir sour cream into salsa
  sauce and spoon over chicken.
  Serves 4 to 5.

Delightful Chicken and Veggies

4–5 boneless, skinless
  chicken breast halves
1 425-g (15-ounce) can corn
  kernels, drained
280 g (10 ounces) frozen
  green peas, thawed
1 455-g (16-ounce) jar
  alfredo sauce
1 teaspoon chicken
  seasoning
1 teaspoon minced garlic
Pasta, cooked

- Brown chicken in frypan and
  place in sprayed, oval
  slow cooker.

- Combine corn, peas, alfredo
  sauce, ¼ cup (60 ml) water,
  chicken seasoning and minced
  garlic in bowl and spoon mixture
  over chicken.

- Cover and cook on low for
  4 to 5 hours. Serve over pasta.
  Serves 4 to 5.

Slow Cooker Cordon Bleu

**4 boneless, skinless chicken
breast halves
4 slices cooked ham
4 slices Swiss cheese,
softened
1 280-g (10-ounce) can cream
of chicken soup
¼ cup (60 ml) milk
Noodles, cooked**

- Place chicken on cutting board and pound until breast halves are thin.

- Place ham and cheese slices on chicken, roll and secure with toothpick.

- Arrange chicken rolls in sprayed 4-L (4-quart) slow cooker.

- Pour chicken soup with milk into saucepan, heat just enough to mix well and pour over chicken rolls.

- Cover and cook on low for 4 to 5 hours.

- Serve over noodles and cover with sauce from soup. Serves 4.

Delicious Chicken Pasta

455-g (1 pound) chicken tenders
Lemon-herb chicken seasoning
3 tablespoons (40 g) butter
1 onion, coarsely chopped
1 425-g (15-ounce) can diced
   tomatoes
1 280-g (10-ounce) can
   mushroom soup
230 g (8 ounces) angel
   hair pasta

- Pat chicken dry with several paper towels and sprinkle ample amount of chicken seasoning.

- Melt butter in large frypan, brown chicken and place in oval slow cooker. Pour remaining butter and seasonings over chicken and cover with onion.

- In separate bowl, combine tomatoes and mushroom soup and pour over chicken and onions. Cover and cook on low for 4 to 5 hours.

- When ready to serve, cook pasta according to package directions. Serve chicken and sauce over pasta. Serves 4.

Farmhouse Dinner

1 230-g (8-ounce) package
   fettuccini (medium egg
   noodles)
4–5 boneless, skinless
   chicken breast halves
Canola oil
½ litre carton chicken stock
2 cups (200 g) sliced celery
2 onions, chopped
1 green capsicum,
   seeded, chopped
1 red capsicum, seeded, chopped
1 280-g (10-ounce) can cream
   of chicken soup
1 280-g (10-ounce) can cream
   of mushroom soup
1 cup (115 g) shredded
   cheddar cheese blend

- Cook pasta in boiling water until barely tender and drain well.

- Cut chicken into thin slices and brown lightly in frypan with a little oil.

- Mix pasta, chicken and stock in large, sprayed slow cooker.

- Make sure pasta separates and coat with stock. Stir in remaining ingredients.

- Cover and cook on low for 4 to 6 hours. Serves 4 to 5.

Golden Chicken Dinner

5 boneless, skinless
   chicken breast halves
6 medium new (red)
   potatoes with peels, cubed
6 medium carrots, chopped
1 tablespoon (15 ml) dried
   parsley flakes
1 teaspoon seasoned salt
1 280-g (10-ounce) can
   mushroom soup
1 280-g (10-ounce) can cream
   of chicken soup
4 tablespoons (15 g) dried
   mashed potato flakes
Water or milk

- Cut chicken into 1.2-cm (½-inch) pieces.

- Place potatoes and carrots in slow cooker and top with chicken breasts.

- Sprinkle parsley flakes, seasoned salt and ½ teaspoon pepper over chicken. Combine soups in bowl and spread over chicken.

- Cover and cook on low for 6 to 7 hours.

- Stir in potato flakes and a little water or milk if necessary to make gravy and cook for an additional 30 minutes. Serves 4 to 6.

Hawaiian Chicken

6 boneless, skinless chicken
  breast halves
1 425-g (15-ounce) can pineapple
  slices with juice
⅓ cup (75 g) brown sugar
2 tablespoons (30 ml) lemon juice
¼ teaspoon ground ginger
¼ cup (30 g) cornflour
Rice, cooked

- Place chicken in sprayed, oval slow cooker and sprinkle with a little salt. Place pineapple slices over chicken.

- Combine pineapple juice, brown sugar, lemon juice, ginger and cornflour in small bowl and stir until cornflour mixes with liquids. Pour over chicken.

- Cover and cook on low for 4 to 5 hours or on high for 2 hours 30 minutes to 3 hours. Serve over rice. Serves 4 to 6.

Imperial Chicken

170 g (6 ounces) instant
  chicken-flavoured rice
1 455-g (16-ounce) jar
  three-cheese pasta bake sauce
6 boneless, skinless
  chicken breast halves
455 g (16 ounces) frozen
  French-style green
  beans, thawed
½ cup (85 g) slivered almonds,
  toasted

- Combine 2½ cups (625 ml) water, rice and seasoning packet into sprayed, oval slow cooker and stir well.

- Spoon in cheese sauce and mix well. Place chicken in slow cooker and cover with green beans.

- Cover and cook on low for 3 to 5 hours. When ready to serve, sprinkle with slivered almonds. Serves 4 to 6.

Here's the Stuff

**5 boneless, skinless chicken
    breast halves
2 280-g (10-ounce) cans
    cream of chicken soup
170 g (6 ounces)
    chicken stuffing mix
455 g (16 ounces) frozen
    green peas, thawed**

- Place chicken in 6-L (6-quart) slow cooker and spoon soups over chicken.

- Combine stuffing mix with ingredients on package directions, include seasoning packet in bowl and spoon over chicken and soup.

- Cover and cook on low for 5 to 6 hours.

- Sprinkle drained green peas over top of stuffing. Cover and cook for an additional 45 to 50 minutes. Serves 4 to 5.

Mushroom Chicken

4 boneless, skinless
chicken breast halves
1 425-g (15-ounce) can
tomato soup
2 115-g (4-ounce) cans
sliced mushrooms,
drained
1 chopped onion
1 chopped green capsicum
1 chopped red capsicum
2 teaspoons Italian seasoning
1 teaspoon minced garlic

- Brown chicken in frypan and place in oval slow cooker.

- Combine tomato soup, mushrooms, onion and capsicums, Italian seasoning, garlic and ¼ cup (60 ml) water in bowl and spoon over chicken.

- Cover and cook on low for 4 to 5 hours. Serves 4.

Orange Chicken

6 boneless, skinless
    chicken breast halves
1 340-g (12-ounce) jar
    orange marmalade
1 230-g (8-ounce) bottle
    Thousand Island
    salad dressing
30 g (1 ounce) onion soup mix

- Place chicken in oval slow cooker. Combine orange marmalade, dressing, soup mix and ¾ cup (175 ml) water in bowl and stir well.

- Spoon mixture over chicken. Cover and cook on low for 4 to 6 hours. Serves 4 to 6.

Oregano Chicken

½ cup (115 g) butter, melted
30 g (1 ounce) Italian salad
    dressing
1 tablespoon (15 ml) lemon juice
4–5 boneless, skinless
    chicken breast halves
2 tablespoons (30 ml) dried
    oregano

- Combine butter, dressing and lemon juice in bowl and mix well.

- Place chicken in large, sprayed slow cooker. Spoon butter-lemon juice mixture over chicken.

- Cover and cook on low for 5 to 6 hours.

- One hour before serving, baste chicken with pan juices and sprinkle oregano over chicken. Serves 4 to 6.

Quick-Fix Chicken

4–6 boneless, skinless
    chicken breast halves
230 g (8 ounces) sour cream
¼ cup (60 ml) soy sauce
2½ cups (600 ml) French
    onion soup

- Wash and dry chicken with paper towels and place in sprayed, oval slow cooker.

- Combine sour cream, soy sauce and onion soup in bowl, stir and mix well. Add to slow cooker.

- Cover and cook on low for 5 to 6 hours if chicken breasts are large, 3 to 4 hours if breasts are medium. Serves 4 to 6.

TIP: Serve chicken and sauce with hot, buttered rice or mashed potatoes.

Picante Chicken

4 boneless, skinless
    chicken breast halves
1 green capsicum, seeded,
    cut in rings
1 455-g (16-ounce) jar taco
    sauce
⅓ cup (75 g) brown sugar
1 tablespoon (15 ml) mustard

- Place chicken in slow cooker with capsicum rings over top of chicken.

- Combine taco sauce, brown sugar and mustard in bowl and spoon over top of chicken.

- Cover and cook on low for 4 to 5 hours. Serves 4.

Perfect Chicken Breasts

70 g (2.5 ounces) beef jerky
6 small boneless,
  skinless chicken
  breast halves
6 slices bacon
2 280-g (10-ounce) cans
  mushroom soup

- Line bottom of oval slow cooker with slices of beef jerky and overlap some.

- Roll each chicken breast with slice of bacon and secure with toothpick. Place in slow cooker, overlapping as little as possible.

- Combine mushroom soup and ½ cup (125 ml) water or milk in bowl and spoon over chicken.

- Cover and cook on low for 6 to 8 hours. Serves 4 to 6.

TIP: When cooked, you will have a great 'gravy' that is wonderful served over noodles or rice.

Russian Chicken

1 230-g (8-ounce) bottle
   Thousand Island salad
   dressing
1 455-g (16-ounce) can whole
   cranberry sauce
30 g (1 ounce) onion soup mix
4 chicken quarters, skinned
Rice, cooked

- Combine salad dressing,
  cranberry sauce, ½ cup (125 ml)
  water and soup mix in bowl. Stir
  well to get all lumps out of soup
  mix.

- Place 4 chicken pieces in
  sprayed, 6-L (6-quart) oval slow
  cooker and spoon dressing-
  cranberry mixture over chicken.

- Cover and cook on low for 4
  to 5 hours. Serve sauce and
  chicken over rice. Serves 4 to 6.

TIP: Use 6 chicken breasts if
   you don't want to cut up
   a chicken.

So-Good Chicken

4–5 boneless, skinless
   chicken breast halves
1 280-g (10-ounce) can mushroom
   soup
1 cup (250 ml) white cooking
   wine
230 g (8 ounces) sour cream

- Wash, dry chicken breasts with
  paper towels and sprinkle a little
  salt and pepper over each.

- Combine mushroom soup,
  wine and sour cream in bowl
  and mix well. Spoon over
  chicken breasts.

- Cover and cook on low for
  5 to 7 hours. Serves 4 to 6.

Winter Dinner

455 g (1 pound) chicken
    tenderloins
Canola oil
455 g (1 pound) Polish sausage,
    cut in 2.5-cm (1-inch)
    pieces
2 onions, chopped
1 795-g (28-ounce) can baked
    beans with ham sauce
1 425-g (15-ounce) can
    borlotti beans, drained
1 425-g (15-ounce) can
    cannellini beans
1 425-g (15-ounce) can butter
    beans, drained
1 cup (270 g) tomato sauce
1 cup (220 g) brown sugar
1 tablespoon (15 ml) vinegar
6 slices bacon, cooked, crumbled

- Brown chicken slices in a little oil in frypan and place in large, sprayed slow cooker. Add sausage, onions, 4 cans beans, tomato sauce, brown sugar and vinegar and stir gently.

- Cover and cook on low for 7 to 8 hours or on high for 3 hours 30 minutes to 4 hours.

- When ready to serve, sprinkle crumbled bacon over top. Serves 4 to 6.

Savoury Chicken Fettuccini

**910 g (2 pounds) boneless,
  skinless chicken
  thighs, cubed**
½ teaspoon garlic powder
**1 red capsicum,
  seeded, chopped**
2 sticks celery, chopped
**1 280-g (10-ounce) can cream
  of celery soup**
**1 280-g (10-ounce) can cream
  of chicken soup**
**230 g (8 ounces) cubed
  Cheddar cheese**
1 diced roasted red capsicum
**455 g (16 ounces) spinach
  fettuccini (medium
  egg noodles)**

- Place cubed chicken pieces in slow cooker. Sprinkle with garlic powder, ½ teaspoon (2 ml) pepper, capsicum and celery. Top with soups.

- Cover and cook on high for 4 to 6 hours or until chicken juices are clear. Stir in cheese and roasted red capsicum. Cover and cook until cheese melts.

- Cook pasta according to package directions and drain. Place pasta in serving bowl and spoon chicken over pasta. Serve hot. Serves 4 to 6.

Scrumptious Chicken Breasts

There is a lot of delicious sauce.

**5–6 boneless, skinless
chicken breast halves
1 teaspoon chicken seasoning
1 280-g (10-ounce) can cream
of chicken soup
1 280-g (10-ounce) can
cream of celery soup
½ cup (125 ml) white
cooking wine
Noodles, cooked**

- Place breast halves, sprinkled with black pepper and chicken seasoning, in sprayed oval slow cooker.

- Combine soups and wine in saucepan and heat enough to mix well. Pour over chicken.

- Cover and cook on low for 5 to 6 hours.

- Serve chicken and sauce over noodles. Serves 4 to 6.

TIP: If chicken breasts are very large, cut in half lengthwise. This is great served with roasted garlic, oven-baked focaccia.

Smothered Chicken Breasts

**4 boneless, skinless
    chicken breast halves**
**1½ cups (300 ml) French
    onion soup**
2 teaspoons chicken seasoning
**1 115-g (4-ounce) jar sliced
    mushrooms, drained**
**1 cup (115 g) shredded
    mozzarella cheese**
Chopped spring onions

- Brown chicken in frypan and place in sprayed, oval slow cooker.

- Pour onion soup over chicken and sprinkle black pepper and chicken seasoning over chicken.

- Place mushrooms and cheese over chicken.

- Cover and cook on low for 4 to 5 hours. To give this chicken a really nice touch when ready to serve, sprinkle some chopped spring onions over each serving. Serves 4.

Southwestern Chicken Pot

6 boneless, skinless
  chicken breast halves
1 teaspoon ground cumin
1 teaspoon chilli powder
1 280-g (10-ounce) can cream
  of chicken soup
1 280-g (10-ounce) can cream
  of celery soup
1 cup (265 g) salsa
Rice, cooked
Flour tortillas

• Sprinkle chicken breasts with
  cumin, chilli powder and a little
  salt and pepper and place in
  sprayed, oval slow cooker.

• Combine soups and salsa in
  saucepan. Heat just enough
  to mix and pour over chicken.

• Cover and cook on low for
  6 to 7 hours. Serve over rice
  with warmed, flour tortillas
  spread with butter.
  Serves 4 to 6.

Sweet-and-Sour Chicken

6 boneless, skinless
  chicken breast halves
Canola oil
30 g (1 ounce) onion soup mix
½ cup (125 ml) orange cordial

• Brown chicken in little oil
  in frypan and place in large,
  sprayed slow cooker.

• Combine onion soup mix,
  orange cordial and ½ cup
  (125 ml) water in bowl
  and pour over chicken.

• Cover and cook on low for
  3 to 5 hours. Serves 4 to 6.

Sunday Chicken

**4 large boneless, skinless
    chicken breast halves
Chicken seasoning
4 slices Colby cheese
1 280-g (10-ounce) can cream
    of celery soup
½ cup (120 g) sour cream
170 g (6 ounces) chicken
    stuffing mix
½ cup (115 g) butter, melted**

- Wash and dry chicken with paper towels and place in sprayed, oval slow cooker. Sprinkle each breast with chicken seasoning.

- Place slice of cheese over each chicken breast.

- Combine celery soup and sour cream in bowl, mix well and spoon over chicken and cheese.

- Sprinkle chicken stuffing mix over top of cheese. Drizzle melted butter over stuffing mix.

- Cover and cook on low for 5 to 6 hours. Serves 4.

Tasty Chicken-Rice and Veggies

4 boneless, skinless chicken breast halves
2 280-g (10-ounce) jars sweet-and-sour sauce
455 g (16 ounces) frozen broccoli florets, cauliflower and carrots, thawed
280 g (10 ounces) frozen green peas, thawed
2 cups (200 g) sliced celery
170 g (6 ounces) instant chicken-flavoured rice
⅓ cup (55 g) toasted, slivered almonds

- Cut chicken in 2.5-cm (1-inch) strips.

- Combine pieces, sweet-and-sour sauce and all vegetables in sprayed 6-L (6-quart) slow cooker.

- Cover and cook on low for 4 to 6 hours.

- When ready to serve, cook chicken-flavoured rice according to package directions and fold in almonds.

- Serve chicken and vegetables over rice. Serves 4.

Honey-Baked Chicken

2 small fryer chickens, quartered
½ cup (115 g) butter, melted
⅔ cup (230 g) honey
¼ cup (60 g) Dijon-style mustard
1 teaspoon curry powder

- Place chicken in large slow cooker, skin-side up and sprinkle a little salt over chicken.

- Combine butter, honey, mustard and curry powder in bowl and mix well.

- Pour butter-mustard mixture over chicken quarters.

- Cover and cook on low for 6 to 8 hours. Baste chicken once during cooking. Serves 6 to 8.

Tangy Chicken

1 large fryer chicken, quartered
2 tablespoons (30 g) butter
½ cup (125 ml) steak sauce
425-g (15-ounce) can stewed tomatoes

- Wash, dry chicken with paper towels and place in large slow cooker.

- Combine butter, sauce and stewed tomatoes in saucepan. Heat just until butter melts and ingredients mix well. Pour over chicken.

- Cover and cook on low for 5 to 6 hours. Serves 4 to 6.

Chicken with Orange Sauce

1 whole chicken, quartered
½ cup (75 g) plus 2 tablespoons
   (30 g) flour
½ teaspoon ground nutmeg
½ teaspoon ground cinnamon
2 large sweet potatoes,
   peeled, sliced
1 230-g (8-ounce) can pineapple
   chunks with juice
1 280-g (10-ounce) can cream
   of chicken soup
⅔ cup (150 ml) orange juice
Rice, cooked

- Wash and dry chicken with paper towels. In bowl combine ½ cup (60 g) flour, nutmeg and cinnamon and coat chicken.

- Place sweet potatoes and pineapple in large, sprayed slow cooker. Arrange chicken on top.

- Combine chicken soup, orange juice and remaining flour in bowl and pour over chicken.

- Cover and cook on low for 7 to 9 hours or on high for 3 to 4 hours. Serve over rice. Serves 4 to 6.

Tasty Chicken and Veggies

1.1–1.4 kg (2½–3 pounds) whole chicken, quartered
455 g (16 ounces) baby carrots
4 potatoes, peeled, sliced
3 sticks celery, sliced
1 onion, peeled, sliced
1 cup (250 ml) Italian salad dressing
⅔ cup (150 ml) chicken stock

- Rinse, dry and place chicken in sprayed 6-L (6-quart) slow cooker with carrots, potatoes, celery and onion.

- Pour salad dressing and chicken stock over chicken and vegetables.

- Cover and cook on low for 6 to 8 hours. Serves 4 to 6.

TIP: When serving, garnish with sprigs of fresh parsley.

'Baked' Chicken

1 cup (200 g) white rice
2 280-g (10-ounce) cans cream of chicken soup
½ litre carton chicken stock
30 g (1 ounce) onion soup mix
1 chicken, quartered

- Place rice in 5 to 6-L (5 to 6-quart) oval slow cooker.

- Combine chicken soup, stock, 2 soup cans water and onion soup mix in saucepan and mix well. Heat just enough to mix ingredients.

- Spoon half over rice and place 4 chicken quarters in slow cooker. Spoon remaining soup mixture over chicken.

- Cover and cook on low for 5 to 6 hours. Serves 4 to 6.

Saffron Rice and Chicken

1 medium-sized chicken,
    quartered
½ teaspoon garlic powder
Canola oil
½ litre carton chicken stock
1 onion, chopped
1 green capsicum, cored,
    seeded, quartered
1 yellow capsicum, cored,
    seeded, quartered
1 roasted red capsicum,
    quartered
⅓ cup (20 g) prepared
    bacon bits
2 tablespoons (30 g) butter,
    melted
145 g (5 ounces) saffron
    yellow rice mix

- Sprinkle chicken with garlic powder and a little salt and pepper.

- Brown chicken in little oil in frypan. Place chicken in sprayed, oval slow cooker and pour stock in slow cooker.

- Combine onion, capsicums, roasted red capsicum and bacon bits in bowl and spoon over chicken.

- Cover and cook on low for 4 to 5 hours.

- Carefully remove chicken from cooker to bowl, stir in butter and rice mix and return chicken to cooker.

- Cover and cook for additional 1 hour or until rice is tender. Serves 4 to 6.

Lemon Chicken

**1.1–1.4 kg (2½–3 pounds)
   chicken, quartered
1 teaspoon dried oregano
2 teaspoons minced garlic
2 tablespoons (30 g) butter
¼ cup (60 ml) lemon juice**

- Season chicken with salt, pepper and oregano and rub garlic on chicken.

- Brown chicken on all sides in butter in frypan and transfer to sprayed, oval slow cooker.

- Add ⅓ cup (75 ml) water to frypan, scrape bottom and pour over chicken.

- Cover and cook on low for 6 to 8 hours.

- At last hour of cooking, pour lemon juice over chicken, finish cooking. Serves 4 to 6.

Chicken Coq au Vin

1 medium-sized chicken,
   quartered, skinned
Canola oil
10–12 small white onions,
   peeled
230 g (½ pound) whole
   mushrooms
1 teaspoon minced garlic
½ teaspoon dried thyme leaves
10–12 small new (red)
   potatoes with peels
1½ cups (375 ml) chicken stock
1 cup (250 ml) burgundy wine
6 bacon slices, cooked,
   crumbled

- Brown chicken in frypan on both sides and set aside.

- Place white onions, whole mushrooms, garlic and thyme in sprayed, oval slow cooker.

- Add chicken, potatoes, chicken stock and a little salt and pepper.

- Cover and cook on low for 8 to 10 hours or on high for 3 to 4 hours.

- During last hour, turn heat to high, add wine and continue cooking.

- Sprinkle crumbled bacon over chicken before serving. Serves 4 to 6.

Chicken Cacciatore

2 onions, thinly sliced
1.1–1.4 kg (2½–3 pounds)
   chicken, quartered
2 170-g (6-ounce) cans
   tomato paste
1 115-g (4-ounce) can sliced
   mushrooms
1½ teaspoons minced garlic
½ teaspoon dried basil
2 teaspoons oregano leaves
⅔ cup (150 ml) dry white
   wine

- Place sliced onions in sprayed, oval slow cooker.

- Wash, dry chicken with paper towels and place in slow cooker.

- Combine tomato paste, mushrooms, garlic, basil, oregano and wine in bowl and pour over chicken.

- Cover and cook on low for 7 to 8 hours or on high for 4 hours. Serves 4 to 6.

Taco Chicken

3 cups (420 g) cooked,
   chopped chicken
30 g (1 ounce) taco seasoning
1 cup (200 g) white rice
2 cups (200 g) chopped celery
1 green capsicum,
   seeded, chopped
2 425-g (15-ounce) cans
   stewed tomatoes
2 teaspoons (10 ml) paprika

- Combine chicken, taco seasoning, rice, celery, capsicum, paprika and stewed tomatoes in bowl and mix well.

- Pour into 5-L (5-quart) slow cooker. Cover and cook on low for 4 to 5 hours. Serves 4 to 6.

TIP: This is a great recipe for leftover chicken.

Tangy Chicken Legs

12–15 chicken legs
⅓ cup (75 ml) soy sauce
⅔ cup (150 g) brown sugar
⅛ teaspoon ground ginger

- Place chicken in sprayed 5-L (5-quart) slow cooker.

- Combine soy sauce, brown sugar, ¼ cup (60 ml) water and ginger in bowl and spoon over chicken.

- Cover and cook on low for 4 to 5 hours. Serves 6 to 8.

Monterey Bake

6 15-cm (6-inch) corn tortillas
3 cups (420 g) leftover cubed
chicken
280 g (10 ounces) frozen
corn kernels
1 425-g (15-ounce) can borlotti
beans with liquid
1 455-g (16-ounce) jar hot
salsa
¼ cup (60 g) sour cream
1 tablespoon (15 ml) flour
3 tablespoons (5 g) snipped
fresh coriander
230 g (8 ounces) shredded
Cheddar cheese

- Preheat oven to 120° C (250° F).

- Cut tortillas into 6 wedges. Place half of tortilla wedges in sprayed slow cooker.

- Place remaining wedges on baking pan, bake for about 10 minutes and set aside.

- Layer chicken, corn and beans over tortillas in cooker.

- Combine salsa, sour cream, flour and coriander in bowl and pour over corn and beans.

- Cover and cook on low for 3 to 4 hours.

- When ready to serve, place baked tortilla wedges and cheese on top of each serving. Serves 4 to 6.

Chicken and Stuffing

1 280-g (10-ounce) can cream
    of chicken soup
2 sticks celery, sliced
½ cup (115 g) butter, melted
3 cups (420 g) cooked, cubed
    chicken
455 g (16 ounces) frozen
    broccoli florets, corn
    and red capsicums
230 g (8 ounces) stuffing mix

- Combine chicken soup, celery,
  butter, chicken, vegetables,
  stuffing mix and ⅓ cup (75 ml)
  water in large bowl.

- Mix well and transfer to
  5 to 6-L (5 to 6-quart)
  slow cooker.

- Cover and cook on low for
  5 to 6 hours. Serves 4 to 6.

*TIP: This is a great recipe for
    leftover chicken.*

Chicken and Everything Good

**2 280-g (10-ounce) cans
cream of chicken soup**
⅓ cup (75 g) butter, melted
**3 cups (420 g) cooked, cubed
chicken**
**455 g (16 ounces) frozen broccoli,
corn and red capsicums**
**280 g (10 ounces) frozen
green peas**
230 g (8 ounces) stuffing mix

- Combine soup, butter and ⅓ cup (75 ml) water in large bowl and mix well. Add chicken, vegetables and stuffing mix and stir well. Spoon mixture into large, sprayed slow cooker.

- Cover and cook on low for 5 to 6 hours or on high for 2 hours 30 minutes to 3 hours. Serves 4 to 6.

Chicken Alfredo

680 g (1½ pounds) boneless, skinless chicken thighs, cut into strips
2 sticks celery, sliced diagonally
1 red capsicum, cored, seeded, julienned
1 455-g (16-ounce) jar alfredo sauce
3 cups (215 g) fresh broccoli florets
230 g (8 ounces) fettuccini or linguine (egg noodles)
115 g (4 ounces) grated parmesan cheese

- Cut chicken into strips.

- Layer chicken, celery and capsicum in sprayed 4 to 5-L (4 to 5-quart) slow cooker.

- Pour alfredo sauce evenly over vegetables.

- Cover and cook on low for 5 to 6 hours.

- About 30 minutes before serving, turn heat to high and add broccoli florets to chicken-alfredo mixture.

- Cover and cook for an additional 30 minutes.

- Cook pasta according to package directions and drain.

- Just before serving pour pasta into cooker, mix and sprinkle parmesan cheese on top. Serves 4 to 6.

Sweet and Spicy Chicken

910 g (2 pounds) chicken thighs
¾ cup (205 g) chilli sauce
¾ cup (165 g) brown sugar
30 g (1 ounce) dry onion
    soup mix
¼ teaspoon cayenne pepper
Rice, cooked

- Arrange chicken pieces in sprayed 5-L (5-quart) slow cooker.

- Combine chilli sauce, brown sugar, dry onion soup mix, cayenne pepper and ¼ cup (60 ml) water in bowl and spoon over chicken.

- Cover and cook on low for 6 to 7 hours. Serve over rice. Serves 4 to 6.

Maple-Plum Glazed Turkey Breast

1 cup (320 g) plum jam
1 cup (250 ml) maple syrup
1 teaspoon mustard
¼ cup (60 ml) lemon juice
1.4–2.3 kg (3–5 pounds)
    boneless turkey breast

- Combine jam, syrup, mustard and lemon juice in saucepan. Bring to the boil, turn heat down and simmer for about 20 minutes or until slightly thick. Reserve 1 cup (250 ml).

- Place turkey breast in slow cooker and pour remaining glaze over turkey.

- Cover and cook on low for 5 to 7 hours.

- When ready to serve, slice turkey and serve with heated, reserved glaze. Serves 6 to 8.

Southern Chicken

1 cup (250 ml) unthickened
    cream
1 tablespoon (15 ml) flour
30 g (1 ounce) chicken
    gravy mix
455 g (1 pound) boneless, skinless
    chicken thighs
455 g (16 ounces) frozen stew
    vegetables, thawed
1 115-g (4-ounce) jar sliced
    mushrooms, drained
280 g (10 ounces) frozen green
    peas, thawed
1½ cups (180 g) bread baking
    mix
1 bunch fresh spring
    onions, chopped
½ cup (125 ml) milk

- Combine cream, flour, gravy mix and 1 cup (250 ml) water in bowl, stir until smooth and pour in large slow cooker.

- Cut chicken into 2.5-cm (1-inch) pieces and stir in vegetables and mushrooms.

- Cover and cook on low for 4 to 6 hours or until chicken is tender and sauce thickens. Stir in peas.

- Combine baking mix, onions and milk in bowl and mix well.

- Drop tablespoonfuls of dough onto chicken mixture.

- Change heat to high, cover and cook for an additional 50 to 60 minutes. Serves 4 to 6.

Italian Chicken

1 small head cabbage
1 onion
1 115-g (4-ounce) jar sliced
   mushrooms, drained
1 medium zucchini, sliced
1 red capsicum, cored,
   seeded, julienned
1 teaspoon Italian seasoning
680 g (1½ pounds) boneless,
   skinless chicken thighs
1 teaspoon minced garlic
2 425-g (15-ounce) cans
   Italian stewed tomatoes
Parmesan cheese

- Cut cabbage into wedges, slice onions and separate into rings.

- Make layers of cabbage, onion, mushrooms, zucchini and capsicum in sprayed 6-L (6-quart) slow cooker.

- Sprinkle Italian seasoning over vegetables. Place chicken on top of vegetables.

- Mix garlic with tomatoes in bowl and pour over chicken.

- Cover and cook on low for 4 to 6 hours. When serving, sprinkle a little parmesan cheese over each serving. Serves 4 to 6.

Asparagus-Cheese Chicken

8–10 boneless, skinless chicken thighs
2 tablespoons (30 g) butter
1 280-g (10-ounce) can cream of celery soup
125-g (4-ounce) block cream cheese
½ cup (125 ml) milk
455 g (16 ounces) can asparagus cuts

- Place chicken thighs in sprayed 5-L (5-quart) slow cooker.

- Combine butter, celery soup, cream cheese and milk in saucepan. Heat just enough for butter to melt and mix well. Pour over chicken.

- Cover and cook on low for 5 to 6 hours.

- Remove cover and place asparagus cuts over chicken and cook for an additional 1 hour. Serves 4 to 6.

Cheesy Chicken and Pasta

1 230-g (8-ounce) package
    pappardelle (wide noodles)
1 280-g (10-ounce) can cream
    of chicken soup
4 cups (560 g) cooked, chopped
    chicken breast
425 g (15 ounces) ricotta
    cheese, softened,
    cut in cubes
230 g (8 ounces) shredded
    mozzarella cheese
1 chopped onion
1 chopped green capsicum
1 chopped red capsicum
2 sticks celery, sliced
1½ cups (375 ml) chicken stock
1 teaspoon white pepper

- Cook pasta according to package directions and drain.

- Place pasta, soup, chicken, ricotta cheese, mozzarella cheese, onion, capsicums, celery and stock in sprayed slow cooker. Stir until ingredients blend well.

- Sprinkle white pepper over top of ingredients and cook on low for 7 to 9 hours or on high for 3 hours 30 minutes. Serves 6.

Stupendous Rice and Chicken

2 280-g (10-ounce) cans cream of chicken soup
230-g (8-ounce) packet instant chicken-flavoured rice
1 red capsicum, seeded, cut into strips
1 green capsicum, seeded, cut into strips
1 115-g (4-ounce) can sliced mushrooms
4–5 boneless, skinless chicken breast halves

- Combine chicken soup, rice, seasoning packet and 2 cups (500 ml) water in large bowl. Pour half mixture into sprayed 4 to 5-L (4 to 5-quart) slow cooker (must be large slow cooker because rice will expand during cooking).

- Layer capsicum strips, mushrooms and chicken on top and pour remaining soup-rice mixture over chicken.

- Cover and cook on low for 6 to 7 hours or on high for 3 to 4 hours. Do not cook any longer than above time as rice will become mushy if over cooked. Serves 4 to 5.

Three Hour Chicken

1 280-g (10-ounce) can cream
    of chicken soup
1 115-g (4-ounce) can sliced
    mushrooms
1 small onion, finely chopped
1 teaspoon Italian seasoning
680 g (1½ pounds) skinless,
    boneless chicken
    breasts, cut in strips
Rice, cooked

- Combine soup, mushrooms,
  onion and seasoning in
  sprayed slow cooker. Add
  chicken strips.

- Cover and cook on low for 2
  hours 30 minutes to 3 hours.
  Serve over rice. Serves 4.

Arroz con Pollo

1360 g (3 pounds) chicken thighs
2 425-g (15-ounce) cans
    Italian stewed tomatoes
455 g (16 ounces) frozen
    green peas, thawed
2 cups (370 g) long grain rice
10 g (0.28 ounces) yellow rice
    seasoning mix
1 litre carton chicken stock
1 heaped teaspoon
    minced garlic
1 teaspoon dried oregano

- Combine all ingredients plus
  ¾ cup (175 ml) water in large,
  sprayed slow cooker and
  stir well.

- Cover and cook on low for
  7 to 8 hours or on high for
  3 hours 30 minutes to 4 hours.
  Serves 6 to 8.

Yes to This Chicken

5–6 boneless, skinless
   chicken breast halves
1 230-g (8-ounce) bottle
   Italian-style
   salad dressing
1½ cups (375 ml) chicken stock
1 310-g (11-ounce) can
   corn kernels, drained
1 red capsicum, finely chopped
230 g (8 ounces) shredded
   cheddar cheese
¾ teaspoon dried basil
340 g (12 ounces) pasta

- Place chicken in sprayed, oval slow cooker. Pour salad dressing over chicken. Cover and cook on low for 6 to 8 hours.

- Drain juices from slow cooker and stir in stock, corn, capsicum, cheese, basil and a little salt and pepper. Combine and cook on low for an additional 1 hour.

- Cook your favourite pasta, drain and place on serving platter. Place chicken over pasta and spoon mixture over chicken breasts. Serves 5 to 6.

Turkey Bake

680 g (1½ pounds) turkey tenderloins
170 g (6 ounces) instant Chinese rice
280 g (10 ounces) frozen green peas, thawed
1 cup (100 g) sliced celery
¼ cup (60 g) butter, melted
½ litre carton chicken stock
1½ cups (105 g) fresh broccoli florets

- Cut turkey into strips. Sauté turkey strips in non-stick frypan until it is no longer pink.

- Combine turkey strips, rice mix plus seasoning packet, peas, celery, butter, chicken stock and 1 cup (250 ml) water in large slow cooker and mix well.

- Cover and cook on low for 4 to 5 hours. Turn heat to high setting, add broccoli and cook for an additional 20 minutes. Serves 4 to 6.

Turkey Loaf

910 g (2 pounds) minced turkey
1 onion, very finely chopped
½ red capsicum, very
**   finely chopped**
2 teaspoons minced garlic
½ cup (135 g) chilli sauce
2 large eggs, beaten
¾ cup (175 ml) breadcrumbs
1 teaspoon Italian seasoning

- Make foil handles by cutting 3 (8 x 45-cm/3 x 18-inch) strips of heavy foil; place in bottom of slow cooker in crisscross strips (resembles spokes on wheel) up and over sides.

- Combine all ingredients plus 1 teaspoon salt and ½ teaspoon pepper in large bowl and mix well.

- Shape into round loaf and place on top foil. Fold extended strips over food. When finished cooking, lift food out by handles.

- Cover and cook on low for 5 to 6 hours. Serves 4 to 6.

Turkey Spaghetti

910 g (2 pounds) minced turkey
2 280-g (10-ounce) cans
   tomato condensed soup
½ litre carton chicken stock
400 g (14 ounces) spaghetti,
   broken, cooked, drained
1 425-g (15-ounce) can
   corn kernels, drained
1 115-g (4-ounce) can sliced
   mushrooms, drained
¼ cup (70 g) tomato sauce

- Cook turkey in non-stick frypan and season with a little salt and pepper. Place cooked turkey in 5 to 6-L (5 to 6-quart) slow cooker.

- Add in soup, stock, pasta, corn, mushrooms and tomato sauce and stir to blend.

- Cover and cook on low for 5 to 7 hours or on high for 3 hours. Serves 4 to 6.

Turkey Cassoulet

2 cups (280 g) cooked, cubed
    turkey
230 g (8 ounces) smoked turkey
    sausage meat
3 carrots, sliced
1 onion, halved, sliced
1 425-g (15-ounce) can cannellini
    beans
1 425-g (15-ounce) can butter
    beans
1 230-g (8-ounce) can tomato
    soup
1 teaspoon dried thyme
¼ teaspoon ground allspice

- Cut turkey sausage in 1.2-cm (½-inch) pieces.

- Combine all ingredients in sprayed slow cooker.

- Cover and cook on low for 4 to 5 hours. Serves 4.

TIP: This is a great recipe for leftover turkey.

Colourful Rice and Turkey

1 280-g (10-ounce) can
   cream of mushroom soup
1 280-g (10-ounce) can
   cream of chicken soup
2 cups (200 g) white rice
3 sticks celery, sliced
   diagonally
455 g (16 ounces) frozen
   Oriental vegetable mix
3 cups (420 g) cooked, cubed
   turkey (or chicken)
1 teaspoon chicken seasoning
1 litre carton chicken stock

- Pour mushroom soup and chicken soup in saucepan and add 1 soup can water. Heat just enough to mix well and pour into sprayed 5 to 6-L (5 to 6-quart) slow cooker.

- Add remaining ingredients and mix.

- Cover and cook on low for 5 to 6 hours. Serves 4 to 6.

Sausage and Rice

**455 g (1 pound) turkey
  sausage
170 g (6 ounces) instant flavoured
  rice mix
1 litre carton chicken stock
2 cups (200 g) sliced celery
1 red capsicum, cored,
  seeded, julienned
1 425-g (15-ounce) can cut
  green beans, drained
⅓ cup (55 g) slivered
  almonds, toasted**

- Break up turkey sausage and brown in frypan.

- Place in sprayed 4 to 5-L (4 to 5-quart) slow cooker.

- Add rice, 1 cup (250 ml) water, chicken stock, celery, capsicum and green beans and stir to mix.

- Cover and cook on low for 3 to 4 hours.

- When ready to serve, sprinkle almonds over top. Serves 4.

Pork & Seafood

Chops, Loins, Loaves & Hams

Pork & Seafood Contents

Stuffed Pork Chops

**4–5 2.5-cm (1-inch) thick
  pork chops
1 425-g (15-ounce) can
  mixed vegetables,
  well drained
1 230-g (8-ounce) can corn
  kernels, drained
½ cup (200 g) rice
1 cup (120 g) breadcrumbs
1 teaspoon Italian seasoning
1 425-g (15-ounce) can stewed
  tomatoes, slightly
  drained**

- Cut pocket in each pork chop and season with a little salt and pepper.

- Combine vegetables, corn, rice, seasoning and breadcrumbs in large bowl and stuff pork chops with vegetable mixture. Secure open sides with toothpicks.

- Place remaining vegetable mixture in 5-L (5-quart) slow cooker. Add pork chops and spoon stewed tomatoes over top of pork chops.

- Cover and cook on low for 8 to 9 hours.

- Serve vegetable mixture along with pork chops. Serves 4 to 5.

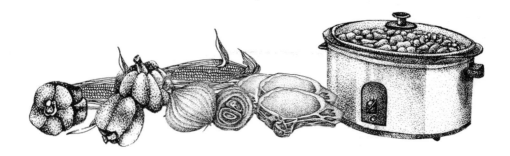

Good Time Chops, Tators and Peas

1 280-g (10-ounce) can
    cream of mushroom soup
1 115-g (4-ounce) can sliced
    mushrooms
5–6 boneless pork chops
Lemon pepper
2 425-g (15-ounce) cans
    whole new potatoes, drained
1 280-g (10-ounce) can
    frozen green peas,
    thawed

- Spoon soup and mushrooms in sprayed slow cooker and stir in ¼ cup (60 ml) water to thin soup slightly.

- Season each pork chop with lemon pepper and place in slow cooker.

- Cover and cook on low for 6 to 8 hours.

- Remove lid and place potatoes and peas around pork chops; turn heat to high and cook for an additional 1 hour 30 minutes. Serves 5.

Smothered Pork Chop Dinner

6 1.8-cm (¾-inch thick)
    bone-in pork chops
8–10 medium red
    (new) potatoes
    with peels
2 onions, sliced
1 280-g (10-ounce) can
    cream of chicken soup
1½ cups (375 ml) chicken stock
¼ cup (60 g) Dijon-style
    mustard
1 teaspoon dried basil leaves

- Brown pork chops sprinkled with a little salt and pepper in non-stick frypan. Place potatoes and onions in 5 to 6-L (5 to 6-quart) slow cooker and add browned pork chops.

- Combine soup, mustard and basil leaves in saucepan. Heat just enough to mix well and pour over pork chops. Cover and cook on low for 7 to 9 hours. Serves 4 to 6.

TIP: To 'dress up' the pork chops, add fried onion rings.

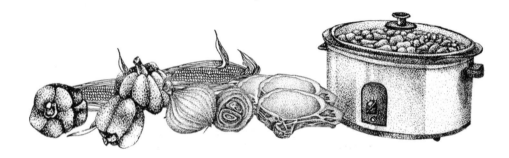

Pork Chops Deluxe

6 2.5-cm (1-inch thick)
   boneless pork chops
1 teaspoon seasoned salt
1 310-g (11-ounce) can
   corn kernels, drained
1 onion, chopped
1 red capsicum, chopped
1 115-g (4-ounce) can sliced
   mushrooms,
   drained, chopped
1¼ cups (150 g) seasoned
   breadcrumbs
1 230-g (8-ounce) can
   tomato soup
2 chopped green chillies

- Cut pocket in each pork chop, cutting from side almost to edge. Season pockets with the seasoned salt.

- In a bowl, combine corn, onions, capsicum, mushrooms and breadcrumbs in bowl. Pack vegetable mixture into pockets and secure along open side with wooden picks.

- Spread any remaining vegetable mixture in sprayed slow cooker. Combine tomato soup and green chillies in bowl and mix well.

- Moisten top surface of each stuffed chop with tomato mixture and place in slow cooker. Pour remaining tomato mixture on top of pork chops.

- Cover and cook on low for 8 to 9 hours or on high for 4 to 5 hours. When ready to serve, remove pork chops to serving platter and mound vegetable mixture in centre. Serves 6.

Savoury Pork Chops

6 1.8-cm (¾-inch thick) pork chops
1 cup (250 ml) pineapple juice
⅓ cup (75 g) brown sugar
3 tablespoons (45 ml) cider vinegar
Noodles, cooked

- Brown pork chops in frypan on both sides and place in 5-L (5-quart) slow cooker.

- Combine pineapple juice, brown sugar and vinegar in bowl and mix well.

- Pour brown sugar-vinegar mixture over pork chops.

- Cover and cook on low for 4 to 5 hours.

- Serve over noodles. Serves 4 to 6.

Ranch Pork Chops

6 1.8-cm (¾-inch thick) bone-in pork chops
10 g (.04 ounces) French onion soup mix
2 425-g (15-ounce) cans new potatoes, drained, quartered
1 280-g (10-ounce) can cream of celery soup

- Place pork chops in sprayed 6-L (6-quart) oval slow cooker.

- Sprinkle pork chops with soup mix and ½ teaspoon pepper.

- Place potatoes around pork chops and pour celery soup around potatoes and chops.

- Cover and cook on low for 4 to 5 hours. Serves 4 to 6.

Pork Chops with Orange Sauce

**2 medium sliced yellow
  squash
2 onions, sliced
6–8 bone-in pork chops
½ cup (125 ml) chicken stock
½ cup (160 g) orange marmalade
1 tablespoon (15 ml)
  honey-mustard
2 tablespoons (15 g) cornflour**

- Place squash and onions in
  5 to 6-L (5 to 6-quart)
  slow cooker.

- Sprinkle a little salt and pepper
  on top of pork chops and place
  over vegetables.

- Combine stock, marmalade and
  mustard in bowl and spoon over
  pork chops.

- Cover and cook on low for
  4 to 6 hours.

- Transfer pork chops and
  vegetables to serving plate and
  cover to keep warm.

- For sauce, pour liquid from slow
  cooker into medium saucepan.
  Combine 2 tablespoons (30 ml)
  water with cornflour and add
  to saucepan.

- Heat mixture, stir constantly
  until thick and serve over pork
  chops and vegetables.
  Serves 6 to 8.

Western Pork Dinner

6 1.8-cm (¾-inch thick)
   boneless pork chops
1 425-g (15-ounce) can chilli
   beans
1½ cups (395 g) salsa
1 green capsicum, chopped
1 onion, chopped
1 red capsicum, chopped
1 125-g (4-ounce) can corn
   kernels
1 115-g (4-ounce) can
   sliced black olives
1½–2 cups (145–190 g) instant
   brown rice
2 tablespoons (30 g) butter,
   melted

- Arrange pork chops in sprayed, oval slow cooker and cover with chilli beans and salsa.

- Cover and cook on low for 5 hours or on high for 2 hours 30 minutes.

- Increase heat to high (if cooking on low) and stir in vegetables and olives. Cover and cook for an additional 30 minutes.

- Cook brown rice according to package directions and stir in melted butter.

- Place on serving platter. Spoon pork chops and vegetables over rice. Serves 6.

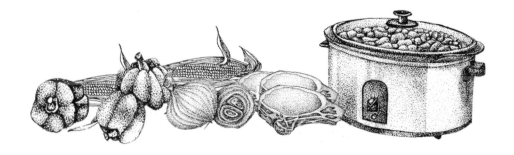

Pork Chops for Dinner

6 1.8-cm (¾-inch thick) pork
    loin chops
1 onion, halved, sliced
1 230-g (8-ounce) can
    tomato soup
¼ cup (55 g) brown sugar
1 tablespoon (15 ml)
    Worcestershire sauce
1 teaspoon seasoned salt

- Brown pork chops in frypan on both sides and place in 4 to 5-L (4 to 5-quart) slow cooker. Place onions over pork chops.

- Combine tomato soup, brown sugar, Worcestershire sauce, seasoned salt and ¼ cup (60 ml) water in bowl and spoon over onions and pork chops.

- Cover and cook on low for 4 to 5 hours. Serves 4 to 6.

Pork Chops and Gravy

6 1.2-cm (½-inch thick) pork chops
8–10 new (red) potatoes with peels, quartered
455 g (16 ounces) baby carrots
2 280-g (10-ounce) cans cream of mushroom soup
1 teaspoon minced garlic

- Sprinkle a little salt and pepper on pork chops.

- Brown pork chops in frypan and place in 5 to 6-L (5 to 6-quart) slow cooker. Place potatoes and carrots around pork chops.

- Heat mushroom soup and garlic with ½ cup (125 ml) water in saucepan and pour over chops and vegetables.

- Cover and cook on low for 6 to 7 hours. Serves 4 to 6.

Pork Chops Pizza

**6 2.5-cm (1-inch) thick
    boneless pork chops
1 onion, finely chopped
1 green capsicum,
    seeded, finely
    chopped
1 230-g (8-ounce) jar pizza
    sauce
280 g (10 ounces) plain couscous
2 tablespoons (30 g) butter
1 cup (115 g) shredded
    mozzarella cheese**

- Trim fat from pork chops and sprinkle with a little salt and pepper. Brown and cook pork chops in frypan on both sides for 5 minutes.

- Transfer chops to sprayed, oval slow cooker. Spoon onion and capsicum over chops and pour pizza sauce over top.

- Cover and cook on low for 4 to 6 hours. Cook couscous according to package directions except add 2 tablespoons (28 g) butter instead of 1 tablespoon (15 ml) and place on serving platter.

- Spoon chops and sauce over couscous and sprinkle cheese over pork chops. Serves 4 to 6.

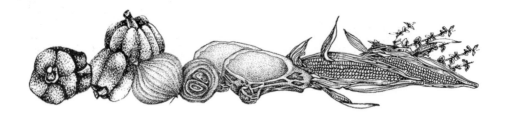

Promising Pork Chops

6 boneless pork chops
115 g (4 ounces) sliced
mushrooms
1 200-g (7-ounce) can tomatoes
2 chopped green chillies
1 280-g (10-ounce) can cream
of mushroom soup
230 g (8 ounces) sour cream
230 g (8 ounces) penne pasta

- Place pork chops in sprayed 5-L (5-quart) slow cooker and layer mushrooms, tomatoes and green chillies over top. Spread mushroom soup with large spoon over top.

- Cover and cook on low for 6 to 8 hours. Transfer pork chops to container that can be kept warm in oven.

- Stir sour cream into sauce in slow cooker and cook on high for about 10 minutes.

- Cook pasta according to package directions.

- Stir pasta into sauce and place pork chops on top. Or if you prefer, place pasta sauce on serving platter and top with warm pork chops. Serves 6.

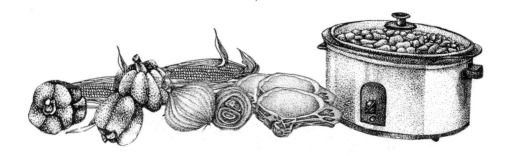

Pineapple-Pork Chops

6–8 1.2-cm (½-inch thick)
   boneless pork chops
Canola oil
½ cup (125 g) pineapple cordial
¼ cup (55 g) brown sugar
⅓ cup (75 ml) wine
⅓ cup (115 g) honey
Rice, cooked

- Brown pork chops in a little oil in frypan and transfer to sprayed slow cooker.

- Combine pineapple cordial, brown sugar, wine and honey in bowl. Pour over pork chops.

- Cover and cook on low for 5 to 6 hours. Serve over rice. Serves 6 to 8.

Peachy Pork Chops

6–8 1.8-cm (¾-inch thick)
   bone-in pork chops
½ cup (110 g)
   brown sugar
¼ teaspoon ground cinnamon
¼ teaspoon ground cloves
1 230-g (8-ounce) can
   tomato soup
1 795-g (28-ounce) can peach
   halves with juice
¼ cup (60 ml) white vinegar

- Brown pork chops in frypan on both sides and place in oval slow cooker.

- Combine brown sugar, cinnamon, cloves, tomato soup, ¼ cup (60 ml) juice from peaches and vinegar in bowl.

- Pour sugar-tomato soup mixture over pork chops and place peach halves over top. Cover and cook on low for 4 to 5 hours. Serves 6 to 8.

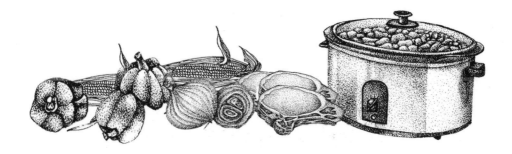

Italian Pork Chops

**6–8 2.5-cm (1-inch) thick
  boneless pork chops**
**230 g (½ pound) fresh
  mushrooms, sliced**
1 onion, chopped
1 red capsicum, chopped
1 green capsicum, chopped
2 teaspoons Italian seasoning
**1 425-g (15-ounce) can
  stewed tomatoes**

- Brown pork chops in frypan and sprinkle with salt and pepper on both sides.

- Combine mushrooms, onion, capsicums and Italian seasoning in 6-L (6-quart) slow cooker and set aside.

- Place pork chops over vegetables and pour stewed tomatoes over pork chops. Cover and cook on low for 7 to 8 hours. To serve, spoon mushroom-seasoning blend over pork chops. Serves 6 to 8.

Honey-Mustard Pork Chops

Try this sauce over hot, cooked rice. It is wonderful!

1 280-g (10-ounce) can mushroom soup
⅓ cup (75 ml) white wine
¼ cup (60 g) honey-mustard
1 teaspoon minced garlic
4–5 1.8-cm (¾-inch thick) pork chops

- Combine soup, wine, honey-mustard, minced garlic and 1 teaspoon salt in large bowl and mix well.

- Place pork chops, sprinkled with a little black pepper in 5-L (5-quart) slow cooker and spoon soup-honey-mustard mixture over chops.

- Cover and cook on low for 5 to 6 hours.

- When ready to serve, lift pork chops out of sauce and onto serving plate. Stir sauce to mix well and serve with pork chops. Serves 4 to 5.

TIP: For a 'meat and potato meal', just slice 3 potatoes and place in slow cooker before adding pork chops.

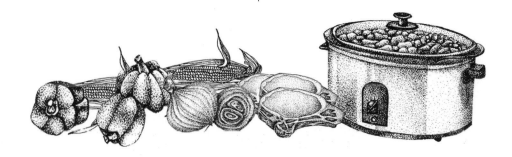

'Baked' Pork Chops

6–8 1.2-cm (½-inch thick) pork chops
Canola oil
1 280-g (10-ounce) can cream of chicken soup
3 tablespoons (50 g) tomato sauce
1 tablespoon (15 ml) Worcestershire sauce
1 onion, chopped

- Brown pork chops in a little oil in frypan and season with a little salt and pepper.

- Place pork chops in sprayed slow cooker.

- Combine chicken soup, tomato sauce, Worcestershire sauce and onion in bowl and pour over pork chops.

- Cover and cook on low for 5 to 6 hours. Serves 6 to 8.

Delicious Pork Chops

1¾ cups (210 g) flour
2 tablespoons (30 ml) mustard powder
8 boneless, thick pork chops
Canola oil
1 280-g (10-ounce) can chicken soup

- Place flour and mustard in shallow bowl. Dredge pork chops in flour-mustard mixture.

- Brown pork chops in a little oil in frypan. Place all chops in 6-L (6-quart) oval slow cooker.

- Pour soup over pork and add about ¼ cup (60 ml) water. Cover and cook on low for 6 to 8 hours. Serves 6 to 8.

Country Pork Chops

7–8 new (red) potatoes
   with peels, sliced
2 onions, sliced
1 280-g (10-ounce) can cream
   of celery soup
⅓ cup (75 ml) chicken stock
3 tablespoons (45 ml)
   Dijon-style mustard
1 115-g (4-ounce) can sliced
   mushrooms, drained
1 teaspoon minced garlic
¾ teaspoon dried basil
8 boneless pork chops
Canola oil

- Place potatoes and onions in large slow cooker.

- Combine soup, stock, mustard, mushrooms, garlic and basil in bowl, mix well and pour over potatoes and onions. Stir to coat vegetables.

- Sprinkle pork chops with a little salt and pepper. Brown pork chops in a little oil in frypan on both sides.

- Place chops over vegetables.

- Cover and cook on low for 6 to 7 hours. Serves 6 to 8.

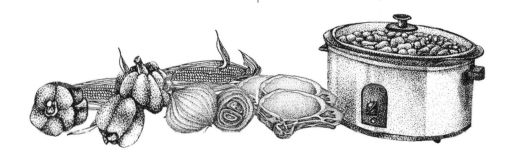

Pork Roast with Apricot Glaze

1.4 kg (3 pounds) boneless
pork roast
⅓ cup (75 ml) chicken stock
1 510-g (18-ounce) jar
apricot jam
2 tablespoons (30 g) Dijon-style
mustard
1 onion, finely chopped
1 green capsicum, seeded,
finely chopped
Rice, cooked

- Trim fat from roast and, if necessary, cut roast to fit into sprayed 4 to 5-L (4 to 5-quart) slow cooker. Place roast in cooker.

- Combine stock, jam, mustard, onion and capsicum in saucepan and heat just enough to mix ingredients well and pour over roast.

- Cover and cook on low for 9 to 10 hours or on high for 5 to 6 hours.

- Transfer meat to serving plate.

- Sauce left in cooker is delicious as is or thicker. To thicken sauce, mix 1 tablespoon (15 ml) cornflour and 2 tablespoons (30 ml) water. Place in saucepan and add sauce from cooker.

- Heat sauce and stir constantly until sauce thickens slightly.

- Sauce may be served with rice or just spoon over roast. Serves 6 to 8.

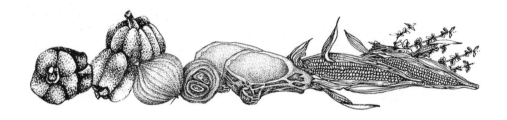

Show Time Pork Roast

2 onions, sliced
1 green capsicum,
    seeded, sliced
1.4 kg (3 pounds) boneless
    pork roast
2 tablespoons (30 ml) soy sauce
1 tablespoon (15 ml)
    tomato sauce
¼ cup (50 g) sugar
3 tablespoons (45 ml) red wine
    vinegar
1 teaspoon minced garlic
340 g (12 ounces) tagliatelle
    (egg noodles), cooked,
    buttered

- Arrange onion and capsicum in sprayed slow cooker; then place roast on top.

- Combine soy sauce, tomato sauce, sugar, vinegar, garlic and a little salt in bowl, mix well and pour over roast.

- Cover and cook on low heat for 6 to 8 hours or on high for 3 to 4 hours. Serve over pasta. Serves 8.

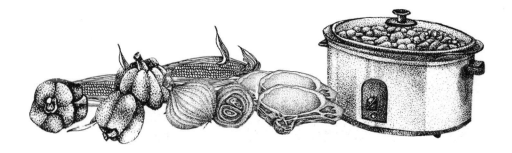

Fruit-Stuffed Pork Roast

1.4–1.6 kg (3–3½ pounds) boneless pork loin roast
1 cup (160 g) mixed dried fruits
1 tablespoon (15 ml) dried onion flakes
1 teaspoon thyme leaves
½ teaspoon ground cinnamon
2 tablespoons (30 ml) canola oil
½ cup (125 ml) apple cider

- Place pork on cutting board. Cut horizontally through centre of pork almost to opposite side. Open pork like a book.

- Layer dried fruits and onion flakes in opening. Bring halves of pork together and tie at 2.5-cm (1-inch) intervals with kitchen twine.

- Combine ½ teaspoon salt, thyme, cinnamon and ½ teaspoon (2 ml) black pepper in small bowl and rub into roast.

- Place roast in frypan with oil and brown roast on all sides.

- Place roast in sprayed slow cooker and pour apple cider in cooker.

- Cover and cook on low for 3 to 4 hours. Partially cool before slicing. Serves 6 to 8.

Pork with a Cranberry Glaze

**1.4–1.8 kg (3–4 pounds)
pork shoulder roast
455 g (16 ounces) frozen
stew vegetables, thawed
1 455-g (16-ounce) can whole
cranberry sauce
2 chopped green chillies
¾ cup (205 g) chilli sauce
1 teaspoon Dijon-style
mustard
2 tablespoons (30 g)
brown sugar**

- Brown roast on all sides in sprayed frypan over medium heat. Place roast in sprayed slow cooker and top with stew vegetables.

- Combine cranberry sauce, green chillies, chilli sauce, mustard and brown sugar in saucepan; heat just enough to blend ingredients. Pour mixture over roast and vegetables.

- Cover and cook on low heat for 8 to 9 hours or on high for 4 to 4 hours 30 minutes. Transfer roast and vegetables to serving platter and keep warm.

- Strain cooking juices and skim off fat. Bring juices to the boil in medium saucepan; reduce heat and simmer for about 25 minutes or until mixture thickens. Serve sauce with sliced pork roast. Serves 6 to 8.

Tender Pork Loin

1.4–1.8 kg (3–4 pounds)
    pork loin
2 teaspoons minced garlic
½ teaspoon rosemary
1 teaspoon sage
1½ teaspoons marjoram

- Place pork in slow cooker,
  rub with minced garlic and
  sprinkle with rosemary, sage and
  marjoram. Add about ¼ cup
  (60 ml) water to slow cooker.

- Cover and cook on low heat for
  4 to 5 hours. Serves 6 to 8.

*TIP: Sometimes it is hard to
    buy a small (1.4 to 1.8-kg/
    3 to 4-pound) pork loin,
    but they are available in
    (3.6 to 4.1-kg/8 or 9-pound)
    sizes. Because pork loin is
    such a good cut of pork
    (no bones–no fat), you can
    buy a whole loin, cut it into
    2 or 3 pieces and freeze the
    pieces not used.*

Terrific Pork Tenderloin

2–3 455-g (1-pound) pork
    tenderloins
1 teaspoon seasoned salt
1 teaspoon garlic powder
2 chopped green chillies
2 280-g (10-ounce) cans
    cream of celery soup
Rice, cooked

- Place pork in sprayed, oval slow
  cooker. Season with seasoned
  salt and garlic powder.

- Combine green chillies
  and celery soup in bowl
  and spoon over pork,
  covering completely.

- Cover and cook on low for
  8 hours. Serve over rice.
  Serves 2 to 3.

Spinach-Stuffed Pork Roast

910 g (2–2½ pounds) pork tenderloin
280 g (10 ounces) frozen, chopped spinach, thawed
⅓ cup (40 g) seasoned breadcrumbs
⅓ cup (35 g) grated parmesan cheese
2 tablespoons (30 ml) canola oil
½ teaspoon seasoned salt

- Cut pork horizontally lengthwise about 1.2 cm (½ inch) from top to within 1.8 cm (¾ inch) of opposite end and open flat.

- Turn pork to cut other side, from inside edge to outer edge, and open flat. If one side is thicker than other side, cover with plastic wrap and pound until both sides are 1.8 cm (¾ inch) thick.

- Squeeze spinach between paper towels to completely remove excess moisture.

- Combine spinach, breadcrumbs and cheese in bowl and mix well.

- Spread mixture on inside surfaces of pork and press down. Roll pork and tie with kitchen twine.

- Heat oil in large frypan over medium-high heat and brown pork on all sides.

- Place in oval slow cooker and sprinkle with salt. Cover and cook on low for 6 to 8 hours. Serves 4 to 6.

Pork and Cabbage Dinner

**455 g (16 ounces)
baby carrots
1 cup (250 ml) chicken stock
30 g (1 ounce) French
onion soup mix
1.4–1.8 kg (3–4 pounds) pork
shoulder roast
1 medium head cabbage**

- Place carrots in 5-L (5-quart) slow cooker.

- Add chicken stock and 1 cup (250 ml) water. Sprinkle dry soup mix and lots of black pepper over carrots.

- Cut roast in half (if needed to fit in cooker) and place over carrot mixture.

- Cover and cook on low for 6 to 7 hours.

- Cut cabbage in small-size chunks and place over roast. Cover and cook for an additional 1 to 2 hours or until cabbage cooks. Serves 6 to 8.

Roasted Red Capsicum Tenderloin

910 g (2 pounds) pork tenderloin
10 g (0.4 ounce) French onion soup mix
1 cup (90 g) roasted red capsicum, rinsed, chopped
230 g (8 ounces) sour cream

- Brown pork in large frypan and place in 6-L (6-quart) oval slow cooker.

- Combine soup mix, capsicum and ½ cup (125 ml) water in bowl and spoon over pork.

- Cover and cook on low for 4 to 5 hours.

- When ready to serve, remove pork from slow cooker.

- Stir sour cream into sauce made. Serve over pork. Serves 4 to 6.

Honey-Mustard Pork Roast

1 green capsicum, seeded, chopped
1 red capsicum, seeded, chopped
2 onions, chopped
3 tablespoons (45 g) honey-mustard
910 g–1.1 kg (2–2½ pounds) pork loin roast

- Combine capsicums and onions in 4 to 5-L (4 to 5-quart) slow cooker. Rub honey-mustard liberally over pork loin with most of honey-mustard on top; place in slow cooker.

- Cover and cook on low for 4 to 6 hours and place in serving platter. Spoon capsicums, onions and pan juices in small serving bowl and spoon over slices of pork to serve. Serves 4 to 6.

Ginger Pork

910 g (2–2½ pounds) boneless
   pork roast
1 cup (250 ml) chicken stock
3½ tablespoons (50 ml)
   quick-cooking
   tapioca or sago
3 tablespoons (45 ml) soy sauce
1 teaspoon grated fresh
   ginger
1 425-g (15-ounce) can pineapple
   chunks with juice
455 g (16 ounces) baby carrots
230-g (8-ounce) can sliced
   water chestnuts,
   drained
Rice, cooked

- Trim fat from pork. Cut pork
  into 2.5-cm (1-inch) pieces,
  brown in large frypan and drain.

- Combine chicken stock, tapioca,
  soy sauce, ginger, pineapple
  juice, carrots and water
  chestnuts in sprayed 4 to 5-L
  (4 to 5-quart) slow cooker. (Chill
  pineapple chunks in refrigerator
  until ready to include in recipe.)

- Add browned pork. Cover and
  cook on low for 6 to 8 hours.

- Turn heat to high and stir in
  pineapple chunks. Cover and
  cook for an additional
  10 minutes.

- Serve over rice. Serves 4 to 6.

Barbecue Pork Roast

Use leftovers for great sandwiches.

1 onion, thinly sliced
2 tablespoons (15 g) flour
910 g–1.4 kg (2–3 pounds)
**   pork shoulder roast**
230-g (8-ounce) bottle
**   barbecue sauce**
1 tablespoon (15 ml)
**   chilli powder**
1 teaspoon ground cumin

- Separate onion slices into rings and place in 4 to 5-L (4 to 5-quart) slow cooker. Sprinkle flour over onions. If necessary, cut roast to fit cooker and place over onions.

- Combine barbecue sauce, chilli powder and cumin in bowl and pour over roast.

- Cover and cook on low for 8 to 10 hours. Remove pork from cooker and slice. Serve sauce over sliced pork. Serves 6 to 8.

TIP: To make sandwiches, shred roast and return to cooker. Cook for an additional 30 minutes to heat thoroughly.

Tangy Apricot Ribs

**1.4–1.8 kg (3–4 pounds)
 baby back pork ribs
1 455-g (16-ounce) jar
 apricot jam
⅓ cup (75 ml) soy sauce
¼ cup (55 g)
 brown sugar**

- Place ribs in large, sprayed slow cooker.

- Combine jam, soy sauce and brown sugar in bowl and spoon over ribs.

- Cover and cook on low for 6 to 8 hours. Serves 6 to 8.

Finger Lickin' Baby Backs

**1.1–1.4 kg (2½–3 pounds) baby
 back pork ribs
½ cup (135 g) chilli sauce
⅓ cup (75 ml) cider vinegar
½ cup (110 g) brown sugar**

- Cut ribs in serving-size pieces, sprinkle with black pepper and place in sprayed 5 to 6-L (5 to 6-quart) slow cooker.

- Combine chilli sauce, vinegar, brown sugar and about ¾ cup (175 ml) water in bowl and pour over ribs.

- Cover and cook on low for about 6 to 7 hours. After about 3 hours, you might move ribs around in slow cooker so sauce is spread over all ribs. Serves 4 to 6.

Delectable Apricot Ribs

1.8–2.3 kg (4–5 pounds) baby back pork ribs
1 455-g (16-ounce) jar apricot jam
⅓ cup (75 ml) soy sauce
¼ cup (55 g) brown sugar
2 teaspoons garlic powder
¼ cup (60 ml) cider vinegar

- Place ribs in sprayed slow cooker.

- Combine jam, soy sauce, brown sugar, garlic powder and vinegar in bowl and spoon over ribs.

- Cover and cook on low for 6 to 7 hours. Serves 8 to 10.

Home-Style Ribs

1.8–2.7 kg (4–6 pounds) boneless pork spare ribs
1 cup (270 g) chilli sauce
1 cup (220 g) brown sugar
2 tablespoons (30 ml) vinegar
2 tablespoons (30 ml) Worcestershire sauce

- Sprinkle ribs liberally with salt and pepper. Place ribs in slow cooker.

- Combine ½ cup (125 ml) water, chilli sauce, brown sugar, vinegar and Worcestershire sauce in bowl and spoon over ribs.

- Cover and cook on low for 5 to 6 hours. Serves 6 to 8.

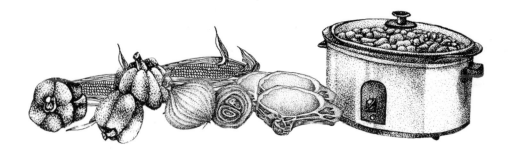

Saucy Ham Loaf

455 g (1 pound) minced ham
230 g (½ pound) minced beef
230 g (½ pound) minced pork
2 eggs, slightly beaten
1 cup (120 g) breadcrumbs
1 teaspoon Italian seasoning
1 145-g (5-ounce) can
  evaporated milk
¼ cup (70 g) chilli sauce
1 teaspoon seasoned salt
115 g (4 ounces) mustard powder
1 cup (250 ml) vinegar
3 eggs, beaten
1 cup (200 g) sugar

- Combine ham, beef, pork, eggs, breadcrumbs, dressing, milk, chilli sauce and salt into a bowl and form into loaf in sprayed, oval slow cooker. Shape loaf so that neither end touches sides of cooker.

- Cover and cook on low for 6 to 7 hours.

- Mix mustard and vinegar in bowl until smooth and let stand overnight.

- Add eggs and sugar and cook in double boiler for 8 to 10 minutes, stirring often or until it coats the spoon. Cool and store in covered jars in refrigerator. Serve over loaf. Serves 4 to 6.

Creamed Ham with Rice

2 280-g (10-ounce) cans cream
  of mushroom soup
2 teaspoons minced garlic
1 cup sliced fresh mushrooms
1 cup sliced red capsicum
2–2½ cups (280–350 g) cooked,
  cubed ham
1 145-g (5-ounce) can
  evaporated milk
1 cup parmesan cheese
Rice, cooked

- Mix together soups, garlic, mushrooms, capsicum, evaporated milk, cheese and a little salt and pepper in slow cooker.

- Cover and cook on low for 2 hours.

- Add cooked rice to slow cooker and toss to coat. Serves 4 to 6.

Walnut Ham

230 g (½ pound) cooked
  ham slices
2 280-g (10-ounce) cans
  cream of celery soup
⅓ cup (35 g) grated
  parmesan cheese
⅔ cup (90 g) chopped
  walnuts
Linguine, cooked

- Cut ham into 1.2-cm
  (½-inch) strips.

- Place soups, cheese, walnuts and
  ham in slow cooker.

- Cover and cook on low for
  1 to 2 hours or until hot
  and bubbly.

- Serve over linguine. Serves 4.

Sweet-and-Sour Sausages

910 g (32 ounces)
  miniature smoked
  sausages
¾ cup (205 g) chilli sauce
1 cup (220 g) brown sugar
¼ cup (55 g) horseradish

- Place sausages in 4-L (4-quart)
  slow cooker.

- Combine chilli sauce, brown
  sugar and horseradish in bowl
  and pour over sausages.

- Cover and cook on low for
  4 hours. Serves 4 to 6.

TIP: This can be served as an
  appetiser or served over hot,
  cooked rice.

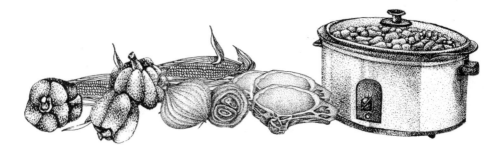

Zesty Ham Dinner

795 g (28 ounces) frozen
   hash browns, thawed
1 onion, chopped
1 red capsicum, chopped
3 cups (420 g) diced
   cooked ham
280 g (10 ounces)
   frozen green peas,
   thawed
2 280-g (10-ounce) cans
   cream of celery soup
1 cup (250 ml) milk
1 bunch fresh spring
   onions, chopped

- Place hash browns, onion and capsicum, ham and peas in sprayed 6-L (6-quart) slow cooker and stir to mix.

- Combine soup and milk in bowl and mix well. Pour over potato mixture and mix well.

- Cover and cook on low for 6 to 8 hours.

- Sprinkle spring onions over top when ready to serve.
Serves 6 to 8.

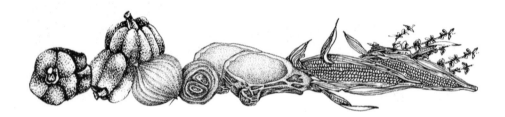

Apricot Ham

**2.7–3.6 kg (6–8 pounds)
shank ham
Whole cloves
2 tablespoons (30 g)
mustard powder
1¼ cups (400 g) apricot jam
1¼ cups (275 g) brown sugar**

- Place ham, fat-side up in slow cooker. Stick lots of whole cloves on outside of ham.

- Combine mustard, jam and brown sugar in bowl and spread all over ham. Cover and cook on low for 5 to 6 hours. Serves 8 to 10.

Ben's Ham and Rice

**170 g (6.7 ounces)
instant flavoured rice
3–4 cups (420–560 g) cooked,
chopped or cubed ham
1 115-g (4-ounce) can sliced
mushrooms, drained
280 g (10 ounces)
frozen green peas
2 cups (200 g) chopped celery**

- Combine rice, seasoning packet, ham, mushrooms, peas, celery plus 2⅔ cups (650 ml) water in 4 to 5-L (4 to 5-quart) slow cooker. Stir to mix well.

- Cover and cook on low for 2 to 4 hours. Serves 4 to 6.

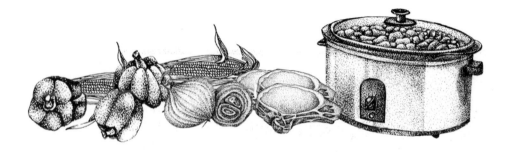

Ham Loaf

Great for leftover ham.

680 g (1½ pounds) cooked, minced ham
455 g (1 pound) minced turkey
2 eggs
1 cup (120 g) seasoned breadcrumbs
2 teaspoons chicken seasoning
1 cup (320 g) cherry jam
2 tablespoons (30 ml) cider vinegar
⅛ teaspoon ground cloves
⅛ teaspoon ground cinnamon

- In bowl, combine ham, turkey, eggs, seasoned breadcrumbs and chicken seasoning in bowl and mix well.

- Use hands to pick up loaf mixture and shape into short loaf that will fit into oval slow cooker.

- Cover and cook on low for 4 to 5 hours.

- Place cherry jam, vinegar, cloves and cinnamon in saucepan and heat. Serve over loaf. Serves 4 to 6.

Special Ham Dinner

2½ cups (350 g) cooked,
  minced ham
⅔ cup (40 g) finely crushed
  cheese crackers
1 large egg
⅓ cup (90 g) hot and spicy
  tomato sauce
¼ cup (60 g) butter
510 g (18 ounces) frozen
  hash browns, thawed
1 onion, coarsely
  chopped
1 145-g (5-ounce) can
  evaporated milk
1½ cups (175 g) shredded
  parmesan cheese
½ teaspoon paprika

- Combine ham, crackers, egg and tomato sauce in bowl and shape into 6 patties.

- Melt butter in frypan and cook hash browns and onion on medium heat for about 10 minutes, turning frequently to prevent browning. Drain and transfer to sprayed slow cooker.

- Combine milk, cheese, paprika and a little salt and pepper in bowl.

- Pour mixture over hash browns and onions. Place ham patties on top; cover and cook on low for 3 to 5 hours. Serves 6.

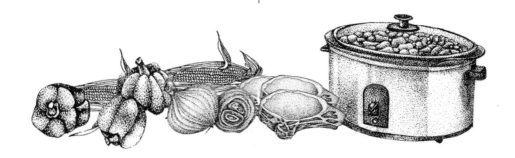

Ham and Potato Dish

4 large baking potatoes, peeled
3 cups (420 g) cubed leftover ham
1 280-g (10-ounce) can corn kernels, drained
1 onion, chopped
1 red capsicum, chopped
1 green capsicum, chopped
1 teaspoon seasoned salt
2 280-g (10-ounce) cans cream of celery soup
125 g (4 ounces) cream cheese
½ cup (125 ml) milk
1 cup fried onion rings

- Cut potatoes into 2.5-cm (1-inch) cubes.

- Combine potatoes, ham, corn, onions, capsicums and seasoned salt in slow cooker.

- Heat cheese, soup and milk in saucepan just enough to mix well. Add to slow cooker and mix with ingredients.

- Cover and cook on low for 5 to 6 hours or until potatoes are tender. When ready to serve, sprinkle onions over top. Serves 4 to 6.

Creamy Potatoes and Ham

5 medium potatoes,
   peeled, sliced
1 onion, chopped
2 cups (280 g) cooked,
   cubed ham
230 g (8 ounces) cubed
   cheddar cheese
1 280-g (10-ounce) can
   cream of celery soup
¼ cup (60 ml) milk

- Layer half each of potatoes,
  1 teaspoon salt, onion, ham
  and cheese in slow cooker and
  repeat layer.

- Combine soup and milk in bowl
  until fairly smooth and add to
  slow cooker.

- Cover and cook on high for
  1 hour. Reduce heat to low and
  cook for 6 to 7 hours. Serves 4.

Creamed Ham with Spaghetti

2 280-g (10-ounce)
   cans cream of
   mushroom soup
2 teaspoons minced garlic
1 cup (70 g) sliced fresh
   mushrooms
2–2½ cups (280–350 g)
   cooked, cubed ham
1 145-g (5-ounce) can
   evaporated milk
200 g (7 ounces)
   spaghetti, broken

- Combine soups, garlic,
  mushrooms, ham, evaporated
  milk and a little salt and pepper
  in slow cooker.

- Cover and cook on low for
  2 hours and mix well.

- Cook pasta in saucepan
  and drain. Add pasta to
  slow cooker and toss to coat.
  Serves 4 to 6.

Ham to the Rescue

2½ cups (350 g) cooked,
     minced ham
⅔ cup (40 g) crushed
     cheese crackers
1 large egg
⅓ cup (90 g) chilli sauce
4 medium potatoes,
     peeled, sliced
Canola oil
1 green capsicum, cored,
     seeded, julienned
230 g (8 ounces) shredded
     cheddar cheese
1 145-g (5-ounce) can
     evaporated milk
1 teaspoon (5 ml) seasoned salt

- Combine ham, crushed crackers, egg and chilli sauce in bowl and mix well.

- Shape ham mixture into 6 patties and set aside.

- Sauté potatoes in a little oil in frypan and turn several times to brown lightly on both sides. Place potatoes and capsicum in 6-L (6-quart) slow cooker.

- In separate bowl, combine cheese, evaporated milk and seasoned salt and pour over potatoes.

- Place ham patties over potatoes.

- Cover and cook on low for 3 to 4 hours. Serves 4 to 6.

Ham and Potato Casserole

3–4 large potatoes, peeled, thinly sliced
230 g (8 ounces) shredded cheddar cheese
½ cup (80 g) chopped onion
½ cup (75 g) chopped green capsicum
2 sticks celery, sliced
2 cups (280 g) cooked, chopped ham
1 280-g (10-ounce) can cream of chicken soup
⅔ cup (150 ml) milk
1 teaspoon seasoned salt

- Place potatoes, cheese, onion, capsicum, celery and ham in sprayed slow cooker and mix well.

- Combine soup, milk and seasoned salt in small bowl and pour evenly over potato-vegetable mixture.

- Cover and cook on high for 4 hours. Serves 8.

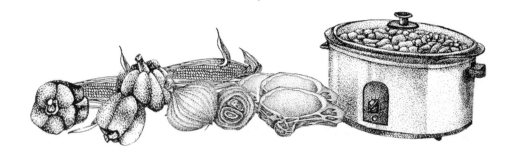

Tortellini Italian-Style

910 g (2 pounds) bulk Italian sausage meat
425 g (15 ounces) tomato pasta sauce
2 cups (145 g) fresh mushrooms, sliced
1 425-g (15-ounce) can Italian stewed tomatoes
1 255 g (9 ounces) refrigerated cheese-filled tortellini
1½ cups (170 g) shredded mozzarella cheese

- Brown and cook sausage meat in frypan for 10 to 15 minutes and drain well.

- Combine sausage meat, pasta sauce, mushrooms and tomatoes in sprayed 5-L (5-quart) slow cooker.

- Cover and cook on low 6 to 7 hours. Stir in tortellini.

- Cover and cook on high for about 15 minutes or until pasta is tender. When ready to serve, sprinkle with cheese. Serves 4 to 6.

Celebrated Sausage and Rice

**455 g (16 ounces) Polish
sausage, cut into 6-mm
(¼-inch) slices
2 425-g (15-ounce) cans
Italian stewed
tomatoes
1 onion, chopped
1 green capsicum, chopped
1 red capsicum, chopped
2 sticks celery, sliced
1 teaspoon Italian seasoning
1 teaspoon dried basil
½ teaspoon hot chilli sauce
1½ cups (145 g) instant rice**

- Layer sausage, stewed tomatoes, onions, capsicums and celery in sprayed slow cooker.

- Sprinkle with Italian seasoning, basil and chilli sauce. Cover and cook on low for 7 hours.

- Stir in rice and ½ cup (125 ml) water and cook for an additional 30 minutes. Serves 4 to 5.

Sausage and Beans

455 g (1 pound) fully cooked smoked sausages
2 425-g (15-ounce) cans baked beans
1 425-g (15-ounce) can cannellini beans, drained
1 425-g (15-ounce) can borlotti beans, drained
½ cup (135 g) chilli sauce
⅔ cup (150 g) brown sugar
1 tablespoon (15 ml) Worcestershire sauce

- Cut sausages into 2.5-cm (1-inch) slices. Layer sausage and beans in slow cooker.

- Combine chilli sauce, brown sugar, a little black pepper and Worcestershire sauce in bowl and pour over beans and sausage.

- Cover and cook on low for 4 hours. Stir before serving. Serves 4.

Sauerkraut and Bratwurst

1 795-g (28-ounce) jar
   refrigerated sauerkraut
¾ cup (175 ml) beer
1 tablespoon (15 ml)
   Worcestershire sauce
30 g (1 ounce) onion
   soup mix
910 g (2 pounds) pre-cooked
   bratwurst

- Combine sauerkraut, beer, Worcestershire sauce and onion soup mix in 4 to 5-L (4 to 5-quart) slow cooker and mix well.

- Cut bratwurst in diagonal slices and place on top of sauerkraut-beer mixture.

- Cover and cook on low for 5 to 6 hours or on high for 2 hours 30 minutes to 3 hours. Serves 4 to 6.

Tuna OK Bake

2 170-g (6-ounce) cans
   tuna, drained, flaked
1 280-g (10-ounce) can cream
   of chicken soup
3 eggs, hard-boiled,
   chopped
3 sticks celery, thinly
   sliced
1 red capsicum,
   seeded, chopped
½ cup (55 g) coarsely
   chopped pecans
½ cup (110 g) mayonnaise
1 teaspoon white pepper
2 cups (110 g) crushed
   potato chips

- Combine tuna, soup, eggs, celery, capsicum, pecans, mayonnaise, white pepper, 1 cup (60 g) potato chips and a little salt in bowl and mix well. Transfer to sprayed slow cooker.

- Cover and cook on low for 5 to 7 hours. When ready to serve, sprinkle remaining potato chips on top. Serves 4 to 5.

Cheddar Crab Casserole

3 tablespoons (45 g) butter
2 sticks celery, thinly
    sliced
1 onion, chopped
1 red capsicum, chopped
4 tablespoons (30 g) flour
1 litre carton chicken stock
1¼ cups (145 g) instant rice
2 170-g (6-ounce) cans
    crabmeat, drained, flaked
1 cup (115 g) shredded
    cheddar cheese
1 115-g (4-ounce) can sliced
    mushrooms, drained
½ cup (95 g) sliced almonds
1 cup (120 g) seasoned
    breadcrumbs
¼ cup (60 g) butter, melted

- Melt butter in frypan on medium heat and lightly sauté celery, onions and capsicums. Add flour and stir well. Slowly add chicken stock, stirring constantly and cook until slightly thickened.

- Combine rice, crabmeat, cheese, mushrooms and almonds in bowl. Stir in sauce and transfer to sprayed slow cooker. Cover and cook on high for 3 to 5 hours.

- Spoon contents of slow cooker into shallow glass serving dish.

- Combine breadcrumbs and melted butter in small bowl; sprinkle over contents in serving dish. Place under griller until crumbs are slightly brown. Serves 5 to 6.

Desserts

Crumbed, Fondued,
Fruited & Fudged

Desserts Contents

Delicious Bread Pudding

8 cups (280 g) cubed leftover
 hot bread rolls
2 cups (500 ml) milk
4 large eggs
¾ cup (150 g) sugar
⅓ cup (75 g) brown sugar
¼ cup (60 g) butter, melted
1 teaspoon vanilla
¼ teaspoon ground nutmeg
1 cup (110 g) finely
 chopped pecans
Caramel topping or
 whipped cream

- Place cubed bread in sprayed slow cooker.

- Combine milk, eggs, sugar, brown sugar, butter, vanilla and nutmeg in bowl and beat until smooth. Stir in pecans. Add to slow cooker.

- Cover and cook on low for 3 hours. Serve with topping or whipped cream. Serves 6.

Bread Pudding with Coconut and Nuts

1 cup (200 g) sugar
½ cup (115 g) butter, softened
1 teaspoon ground cinnamon
4 eggs
3 cups (105 g) white bread cubes
⅓ cup (30 g) flaked coconut
⅓ cup (40 g) chopped pecans

- Beat sugar, butter and cinnamon in bowl. Add eggs and beat well until it blends. Stir in bread, coconut and pecans. Pour into 4 to 5-L (4 to 5-quart) slow cooker.

- Cover and cook on low for 3 to 4 hours or on high 1 hour 30 minutes to 2 hours or until knife inserted in centre comes out clean. Serves 8.

TIP: Serve pudding warm with caramel ice-cream topping, if desired.

Pineapple-Rice Pudding

1 cup (185 g) cooked white rice
¾ cup (150 g) sugar
500 ml (1 pint)
    unthickened cream
1 tablespoon (15 ml) cornflour
3 eggs, beaten
1 teaspoon vanilla
1 425-g (15-ounce) can crushed
    pineapple with juice
Pecans, chopped, toasted

- Combine rice, sugar and cream in bowl and mix well.

- Stir in cornflour, eggs, vanilla and pineapple.

- Pour into sprayed 4 to 5-L (4 to 5-quart) slow cooker.

- Cover and cook on low for 2 to 3 hours.

- When ready to serve, top each serving with toasted, chopped pecans as a special touch. Serves 6.

Baked Apples

4–5 large baking apples
1 tablespoon (15 ml) lemon juice
⅓ cup (40 g) dried cranberries
½ cup (55 g) chopped pecans
¾ cup (165 g) brown sugar
½ teaspoon ground
cinnamon
¼ cup (60 g) butter, melted
Caramel ice-cream topping

- Scoop out centre of each apple and leave cavity about 1.2 cm (½ inch) from bottom.

- Peel top of apples down about 2.5 cm (1 inch) and brush lemon juice on peeled edges.

- Combine cranberries, pecans, brown sugar, cinnamon and butter in bowl. Spoon mixture into apple cavities.

- Pour ½ cup (125 ml) water in oval slow cooker and place apples on bottom.

- Cover and cook on low for 1 to 3 hours or until tender.

- Serve warm or room temperature drizzled with caramel ice-cream topping. Serves 5.

Butter Baked Apples

6 large green baking
   apples
2 tablespoons (30 ml)
   lemon juice
¼ cup (60 g) butter, melted
1 cup (220 g) brown sugar
1 teaspoon ground
   cinnamon
½ teaspoon ground nutmeg
Vanilla ice-cream

- Peel, core, cut apples in half
  horizontally and place in
  slow cooker.

- Drizzle with lemon juice and
  butter. Sprinkle with brown
  sugar, cinnamon and nutmeg.

- Cover and cook on low for
  2 hours 30 minutes to
  3 hours 30 minutes or on high
  for 1 hour 30 minutes to 2 hours.

- Serve with vanilla ice-cream.
  Serves 6.

Peachy-Cranberry Delight

1½ cups (120 g) quick-
   cooking oats
455 g (16 ounces) brown
   sugar
⅔ cup (135 g) sugar
¾ cup (90 g) muffin mix
2 teaspoons ground
   cinnamon
½ cup (125 ml) orange juice
455 g (16 ounces) sliced peaches
170 g (6 ounces)
   dried cranberries

- Combine oats, brown sugar,
  sugar, muffin mix, cinnamon
  and orange juice in large bowl.
  Gently stir in peaches and
  cranberries. Spoon into sprayed
  slow cooker.

- Cover and cook on low for
  5 hours. Serve while still warm.
  Serves 10.

Fresh Peach Cobbler

1 cup (200 g) sugar
¾ cup (90 g) muffin mix
2 eggs
2 teaspoons vanilla
1 145-g (5-ounce) can
    evaporated milk
2 tablespoons (30 g)
    butter, melted
3 large, ripe peaches,
    peeled, mashed
Ice-cream

- Combine sugar and muffin
  mix in large bowl, stir in eggs,
  vanilla, evaporated milk and
  butter and mix well.

- Fold in peaches, pour into
  sprayed slow cooker and
  stir well.

- Cover and cook on low for
  6 to 8 hours or on high for
  3 to 4 hours.

- Serve warm with ice-cream.
  Serves 6.

Peaches with Crunch

¾ cup (60 g) old-fashioned
    oats
⅔ cup (150 g) brown sugar
¾ cup (150 g) sugar
½ cup (60 g) muffin mix
½ teaspoon ground cinnamon
2 425-g (15-ounce) cans
    sliced peaches,
    well drained

- Combine oats, brown sugar,
  sugar, muffin mix and cinnamon
  in bowl.

- Stir in drained peaches and
  spoon into sprayed 3 to 4-L
  (3 to 4-quart) slow cooker.

- Cover and cook on low for
  4 to 5 hours. Serve in small
  dishes. Serves 6.

Cran-Apples for Pound Cake

170 g (6 ounces) dried apples
½ cup dried cranberries
3 cups (710 ml) cranberry juice
¾ cup (180 ml) brown sugar
2 cinnamon sticks, halved
Pound cake or vanilla
  ice-cream

- Add apples, cranberries, juice, brown sugar and cinnamon sticks to sprayed 3 to 4-L (3 to 4-quart) slow cooker.

- Cover and cook on low for 4 to 5 hours or until liquid absorbs and fruit is tender.

- Serve warm, at room temperature or chilled over slices of pound cake or vanilla ice-cream. Serves 6.

Surprise Dessert

510 g (18 ounces) spice
  cake mix
4 eggs, slightly beaten
¾ cup (175 ml) canola oil
100 g (3.4 ounces) butterscotch
  instant pudding mix
230 g (8 ounces) sour cream
1 cup (110 g) chopped pecans
Butter pecan ice-cream

- Combine all ingredients and ¾ cup (175 ml) water in large bowl. Pour into sprayed 4 to 5-L (4 to 5-quart) slow cooker.

- Cover and cook on low for 6 to 7 hours or on high for 3 hours to 3 hours 30 minutes. Serve hot or room temperature with butter pecan ice-cream. Serves 8.

Chocolate Fondue

*Use the slow cooker
as a fondue pot.*

**2 200-g (7-ounce) chocolate
bars, chopped**
**2 60-g (2-ounce) bars
white chocolate,
chopped**
**1½ cups (250 ml)
unthickened cream**
**½ cup (40 g) slivered
almonds, chopped, toasted**
¼ cup (60 ml) amaretto
Pound cake

- Combine broken chocolate bars,
white chocolate bars, cream and
almonds in small, sprayed slow
cooker.

- Cover and cook on low for about
2 hours or until chocolates melt.
Stir to mix well and fold in
amaretto. Serves 6 to 8.

*TIP: Use slow cooker as fondue pot
or transfer chocolate mixture
to fondue pot. Cut pound cake
into small squares and use to
dip into fondue.*

Magnificent Fudge

2 455-g (16-ounce) jars slightly salted, dry-roasted peanuts

340 g (12 ounces) semi-sweet chocolate chips

115-g (4-ounce) bar sweet chocolate, broken

2 680-g (24-ounce) white mint-chip chocolate or 1.4 kg (3 pounds) almond-chip chocolate, chopped

- Place peanuts in sprayed 5-L (5-quart) slow cooker. In layers, add chocolate chips, sweet chocolate and mint-chip chocolate.

- Cover and cook on low for 3 hours without removing lid. After 3 hours, remove lid, stir and cool in covered slow cooker. Stir again and drop teaspoonfuls onto wax paper. Serves 8 to 10.

Chocolate Delight

510 g (18 ounces)
  chocolate cake mix
230 g (8 ounces) sour cream
4 eggs
¾ cup (175 ml) canola oil
100 g (3.4 ounces)
  instant chocolate
  pudding mix
¾ cup (85 g) chopped pecans
Vanilla ice-cream

- Mix cake mix, sour cream, eggs, oil, pudding mix, pecans and 1 cup (250 ml) water in bowl. Pour into sprayed slow cooker.

- Cover and cook on low for 6 to 8 hours. Serve hot or warm with vanilla ice-cream. Serves 8.

Fruit Sauce

8 cups (1.3 kg) fresh fruit,
  thinly sliced
⅓ cup (75 g) brown sugar
⅓ cup (70 g) sugar
2 tablespoons (30 ml)
  quick-cooking
  tapioca or sago
1 teaspoon grated
  fresh ginger
⅔ cup (80 g) dried cranberries
  or cherries
Pound cake or ice-cream

- Combine fruit, brown sugar, sugar, tapioca and ginger in 4-L (4-quart) slow cooker. Cover and cook on low for 4 hours. Add cranberries or cherries and mix well.

- Cover and let stand for 10 to 15 minutes. To serve, spoon over slices of pound cake or ice-cream. Serves 8.

Index

Q

R

S